Data Science

MINDSET, METHODOLOGIES, AND MISCONCEPTIONS

Zacharias Voulgaris, PhD

Technics Publications
BASKING RIDGE, NEW JERSEY

2 Lindsley Road
Basking Ridge, NJ 07920 USA
https://www.TechnicsPub.com

Cover design by Lorena Molinari

Edited by Jessica Lakritz

First Edition

First Printing 2017

Copyright © 2017 Zacharias Voulgaris, PhD

ISBN, print ed.	9781634622561
ISBN, Kindle ed.	9781634622578
ISBN, PDF ed.	9781634622592

Library of Congress Control Number: 2017949255

Contents

Introduction _____ 9

PART 1: Overview of Data Science and the Data Scientist's Work _____ 11

CHAPTER 1: What is Data Science? _____ 13
  Data Science vs. Business Intelligence vs. Statistics _____ 13
    Data Science _____ 13
    Business Intelligence _____ 14
    Statistics _____ 14
  Big Data, Machine Learning, and AI _____ 15
    Big Data _____ 15
    Machine Learning _____ 18
    AI – The Scientific Field, Not the Sci-fi Movie! _____ 18
  The Need for Data Scientists and the Products/Services Provided _____ 20
    What Does a Data Scientist Actually Do? _____ 20
    What Does a Data Scientist Not Do? _____ 21
    The Ever-growing Need for Data Science Professionals _____ 22
  Summary _____ 24

CHAPTER 2: The Data Science Pipeline _____ 25
  Data Engineering _____ 26
    Data Preparation _____ 27
    Data Exploration _____ 28
    Data Representation _____ 28
  Data Modeling _____ 29
    Data Discovery _____ 30
    Data Learning _____ 31
  Information Distillation _____ 32
    Data Product Creation _____ 32
    Insight, Deliverance, and Visualization _____ 33
  Putting It All Together _____ 34
  Summary _____ 35

CHAPTER 3: Data Science Methodologies _____ 37
  Predictive Analytics _____ 37
    Classification _____ 38
    Regression _____ 39
    Time-series Analysis _____ 40
    Anomaly Detection _____ 40
    Text Prediction _____ 41

Recommender Systems_____ 42
   Content-based Systems _____ 43
   Collaborative Filtering _____ 43
   Non-negative Matrix Factorization (NMF or NNMF) _____ 44
Automated Data Exploration Methods _____ 45
   Data Mining _____ 45
   Association Rules _____ 46
   Clustering _____ 46
Graph Analytics _____ 47
   Dimensionless Space _____ 48
   Graph Algorithms_____ 48
   Other Graph-related Topics_____ 50
Natural Language Processing (NLP) _____ 51
   Sentiment Analysis _____ 51
   Topic Extraction/Modeling _____ 52
   Text Summarization _____ 53
   Other NLP Methods_____ 54
Other Methodologies_____ 55
   Chatbots _____ 55
   Artificial Creativity _____ 56
   Other AI-based Methods _____ 56
Summary_____ 58

CHAPTER 4: The Data Scientist's Toolbox _____ 61
Database Platforms _____ 61
   SQL-based Databases_____ 62
   NoSQL Databases _____ 62
   Graph-based Databases _____ 63
Programming Languages for Data Science_____ 64
   Julia _____ 65
   Python _____ 65
   R _____ 66
   Scala _____ 67
   Which Language is Best for You? _____ 67
The Most Useful Packages for Julia and Python_____ 68
Other Data Analytics Software _____ 70
   MATLAB_____ 71
   Analytica _____ 71
   Mathematica _____ 72
Visualization Software_____ 73
   Plot.ly _____ 73
   D3.js _____ 73
   WolframAlpha _____ 74

Tableau _____ 74
Data Governance Software _____ 74
  Spark_____ 75
  Hadoop _____ 75
  Storm _____ 76
Version Control Systems (VCS) _____ 77
  Git _____ 77
  Github_____ 78
  CVS _____ 78
Summary _____ 79

PART 2: Setting the Stage for Data Analytics _____ 81

CHAPTER 5: Data Science Questions and Hypotheses _____ 83
Importance of Asking (the Right) Questions _____ 84
  Formulating a Hypothesis _____ 85
Questions Related to Most Common Use Cases _____ 86
  Is Feature X Related to Feature Y?_____ 87
  Is Subset X Significantly Different to Subset Y? _____ 88
  Do Features X and Y Collaborate Well with Each Other for Predicting Variable Z?___ 89
  Should We Remove X from the Feature Set? _____ 90
  How Similar are Variables X and Y? _____ 91
  Does Variable X Cause Variable Y?_____ 92
  Other Question Types _____ 93
Questions Not to Ask _____ 94
Summary _____ 95

CHAPTER 6: Data Science Experiments and Evaluation of Their Results ____ 97
The Importance of Experiments _____ 97
How to Construct an Experiment _____ 98
Experiments for Assessing the Performance of a Predictive Analytics System _100
A Matter of Confidence _____ 101
Evaluating the Results of an Experiment _____ 103
Summary _____ 105

CHAPTER 7: Sensitivity Analysis of Experiment Conclusions_____ 107
The Importance of Sensitivity Analysis _____ 107
The Butterfly Effect_____ 108
Global Sensitivity Analysis Using Resampling Methods _____ 109
  Bootstrapping _____ 109
  Permutation Methods _____ 110

Jackknife _____ 110
Monte Carlo _____ 111
Local Sensitivity Analysis Employing "What If?" Questions _____ 112
Some Useful Considerations on Sensitivity Analysis_____ 112
Summary _____ 113

PART 3: Common Errors in Data Science_____ 115

CHAPTER 8: Programming Bugs_____ 117
The Importance of Understanding and Dealing with Programming Bugs _____ 117
Places You Usually Find Bugs _____ 118
Types of Bugs Commonly Encountered _____ 119
Some Useful Considerations on Programming Bugs _____ 122
Summary _____ 122

CHAPTER 9: Mistakes Through the Data Science Process _____ 125
How Mistakes Differ From Bugs _____ 125
Most Common Types of Mistakes_____ 126
Choosing the Right Model_____ 129
Value of a Mentor _____ 131
Some Useful Considerations on Mistakes _____ 131
Summary _____ 132

CHAPTER 10: Handling Bugs and Mistakes_____ 133
Strategies for Coping with Bugs _____ 133
Strategies for Coping with High-level Mistakes _____ 135
Preventing Erroneous Situations in the Pipeline _____ 136
Types of Models _____ 136
Evaluating the Data at Hand and Pairing It with a Model_____ 137
Choosing the Right Model for a Classification Methodology _____ 138
Combining Different Options in an Ensemble Setting _____ 139
Other Considerations for Choosing the Right Model_____ 140
Summary _____ 141

PART 4: Other Aspects of Data Science _____ 143

CHAPTER 11: The Role of Heuristics in Data Science _____ 145
Heuristics as Information in the Making _____ 145
Problems that Require Heuristics _____ 146

Why Heuristics are Essential for an AI System _____148
Applications of Heuristics in Data Science _____149
    Heuristics and Machine Learning Processes_____149
    Custom Heuristics and Data Engineering _____149
    Heuristics for Feature Evaluation _____150
    Other Applications of Heuristics_____151
    Anatomy of a Good Heuristic_____151
Some Final Considerations on Heuristics _____153
Summary _____153

CHAPTER 12: The Role of AI in Data Science _____155
Problems AI Solves _____156
Types of AI Systems Used in Data Science _____157
    Deep Learning Networks_____158
    Autoencoders _____159
    Other Types of AI Systems _____160
AI Systems Using Data Science _____161
    Computer Vision _____161
    Chatbots _____162
    Artificial Creativity_____163
    Other AI Systems Using Data Science_____163
Some Final Considerations on AI _____165
Summary _____165

CHAPTER 13: Data Science Ethics _____167
The Importance of Ethics in Data Science _____167
Confidentiality Matters _____168
    Privacy_____168
    Data Anonymization _____170
    Data Security _____171
Licensing Matters _____172
Other Ethical Matters _____173
Some Final Considerations on Ethics_____173
Summary _____174

CHAPTER 14: Future Trends and How to Remain Relevant_____175
General Trends in Data Science _____175
    The Role of AI in the Years to Come _____176
    Big Data: Getting Bigger and More Quantitative_____176
    New Programming Paradigms _____177

The Rise of Hadoop Alternatives _____ 178

Other Trends _____ 178

Remaining Relevant in the Field _____ 179

The Versatilist Data Scientist _____ 179

Data Science Research_____ 180

The Need to Educate Oneself Continuously _____ 181

Collaborative Projects _____ 181

Mentoring _____ 182

Summary_____ 183

Final Words_____ 185

Glossary _____ 187

Index _____ 201

Introduction

A lot of books have been written about data science in the past few years. However, most of these books focus on particular techniques or frameworks (e.g. sci-kit learn package in Python, the Spark framework, or some NoSQL database system), making the whole field seem like a set of methods that need to be memorized in order to get the work done. There is no doubt about the usefulness of all these techniques, yet there is another element that is missing from these strictly technical books: the data scientist mindset and how it is mirrored in the timeless practices that knowledgeable data scientists employ in their work.

In my first book on data science, *Data Scientist: The Definite Guide to Becoming a Data Scientist*, I illustrated the key aspects of this mindset. However, that is a book for those new to data science. In the book that followed, *Julia for Data Science*, I focused on the Julia programming language, a fairly new and promising tool for data science, while I also illustrated many of the most commonly used data science concepts in practice. In this current book, I tackle data science from a different angle, concentrating on the various data science practices that remain relevant throughout time, and how these practices manifest in particular methodologies and systems. Some of the topics in this book are summarized in data science videos hosted on Safari Books Online.

As the data scientist profession has become increasingly popular in the past few years, more and more people have flocked to it. Unfortunately, most of them do not have the time or the proper guidance to delve deep into it, so their aptitude and their mindset in it are limited. Contrary to what many companies say, data science is not something you can pick up in a twelve-week boot camp. To learn it properly, you must dedicate a lot of time to it; perhaps find a mentor who is willing to guide you. You have to invest time researching data science and practicing the various methods, and you need a clear idea of what it offers, what it can deliver, and its requirements. Data science is not a panacea and not all data is created equal. A data scientist who has a mature attitude toward the field applies a holistic approach and as a result does not make promises that can't be kept when it comes to insights and data products.

This book will help you gain a better understanding of the field and organize the various pieces of know-how you may have picked up from other books into a more holistic view of data science. Instead of examining how you can implement all these practices in programming code, this book focuses on concepts and strategies. It is kept as language-agnostic as possible.

Specifically, I cover four different aspects of data science, starting with the data science pipeline and the data scientist's work, including the various methodologies of data science today and the data scientist's toolbox. Even though this kind of information is widely available in a variety of courses on the field, here we look at it from a different angle. We focus on how everything relates to the mindset of the data scientist so that you can learn to pick your tools wisely, as everything described here gives way to new and better technologies.

After a gentle introduction to data science, I go into essential practices which are very important for delving into the data and understanding what it has to offer. This involves detailed questions and hypotheses with regard to data science, accompanied by various examples. Following that, I focus on: bugs and mistakes in the data science process, complete with examples to illustrate each point.

In the fourth section, I look into some other data science aspects that are more general but equally important. These include future trends and how modern technologies like Artificial Intelligence (AI) fit into the data science framework. Also, I take a look into ethics, an important topic that is grossly under-represented in most educational material. Finally, I provide some tips on how you can remain relevant as a data scientist, surviving and even thriving in the ever-changing scenery of the field.

It is my hope that you not only benefit from reading this book and using it as a starting point to explore the topics covered in more depth, but that you find this information inspiring, making your experience in data science more fulfilling and enjoyable.

PART 1

Overview of Data Science and the Data Scientist's Work

CHAPTER 1

What is Data Science?

Data Science vs. Business Intelligence vs. Statistics

Nowadays, a growing number of people talk about data science and its various merits. However, many people have a hard time distinguishing it from business intelligence and statistics. What's worse, some people who are adept at these other fields market themselves as data scientists, since they fail to see the difference and expect the hiring managers to be equally ignorant on this matter. However, despite the similarities among these three fields, data science is quite different, both in terms of the processes involved, the domain, and the skills required. Let's take a closer look at these three fields.

Data Science

Data science can be seen as the interdisciplinary field that deals with the creation of insights or data products from a given set of data files (usually in unstructured form), using analytics methodologies. The data it handles is often what is commonly known as "big data," although it is often applied to conventional data streams, such as the ones usually encountered in the databases, the spreadsheets, and the text documents of a business. We'll take a closer look into big data in the next section.

Data science is not a guaranteed tool for finding the answers to the questions we have about the data, though it does a good job at shedding some light on what we are investigating. For example, we may be interested in figuring out the answer to "How can we predict customer attrition based on the demographics data we have on them?" This is something that may not be possible with that data alone. However, investigating the data may help us come up with other questions, like "Can demographics data supplement a prediction system of attrition, based on the orders they have made?" Also, it is as good as the data we have, so it doesn't make sense to expect breathtaking insights if the data we have is of low quality.

Business Intelligence

As for business intelligence, although it too deals with business data (almost exclusively), it does so through rudimentary data analysis methods (mainly statistics), data visualization, and other techniques, such as reports and presentations, with a focus on business applications. Also, it handles mainly conventional sized data, almost always structured, with little to no need for in-depth data analytics. Moreover, business intelligence is primarily concerned with getting useful information from the data and doesn't involve the creation of data products (unless you count fancy plots as data products).

Business intelligence is not a kind of data science, nor is it a scientific field. Business intelligence is essential in many organizations, but if you are after hard-to-find insights or have challenging data streams in your company's servers, then business intelligence is not what you are after. Nevertheless, business intelligence is not completely unrelated to data science either. Given some training and a lot of practice, a business intelligence analyst can evolve into a data scientist.

Statistics

Statistics is a field that is similar to data science and business intelligence, but it has its own domain. Namely, it involves doing basic manipulations on a set of data (usually tidy and easy to work with) and applying a set of tests and models to that data. It's like a conventional vehicle that you drive on city roads. It does a decent job, but you wouldn't want to take that vehicle to the country roads or off-road. For this kind of terrain you'll need something more robust and better-equipped for messy data: data science. If you have data that comes straight from a database, it's fairly clean, and all you want to do is create a simple regression model or check to see if February sales are significantly different from January sales, analyzing statistics will work. That's why statisticians remain in business, even if most of the methods they use are not as effective as the techniques a data scientist employs.

Scientists make use of statistics, though it is not formally a scientific field. This is an important point. In fact, even mathematicians look down on the field of statistics, for the simple reason that it fails to create robust theories that can be generalized to other aspects of Mathematics. So, even though statistical techniques are employed in various areas, they are inherently inferior to most principles of Mathematics and of Science. Also, statistics is not a fool-proof framework when it comes to drawing inferences about the data. Despite the confidence metrics it provides, its results are only as good as the assumptions it makes about the distribution of each variable, and how well these assumptions hold. This is why many scientists also employ simulation methods to ensure that the conclusion their statistical models come up with are indeed viable and robust enough to be used in the real world.

Big Data, Machine Learning, and AI

Big Data

Big data can mean a wide variety of things, depending on who you ask. For a data architect, for example, big data may be what is usually used in a certain kind of database, while for the business person, it is a valuable resource that can have a positive effect on the bottom line. For the data scientist, big data is our *prima materia*, the stuff we need to work with through various methods to extract useful and actionable information from it. Or as the Merriam Webster dictionary defines it, "an accumulation of data that is too large and complex for processing by traditional database management tools." Whatever the case, most people are bound to agree that it's a big deal, since it promises to solve many business problems, not to mention even larger issues (e.g. climate change or the search for extra-terrestrial life). It is not clear how big data came to get so much traction so quickly, but one thing is for certain: those who knew about it and knew how to harness its potential in terms of information could make changes wherever they were. The people who were the first to systematically study big data and define it as a kind of resource were:

- directly responsible for the development of data science as an independent field
- adept at the data-related problems organizations faced (and are still facing to some extent)
- knowledgeable about data in general

This may sound obvious, but remember that back in the early 2000s, it was only data architects, experienced software developers, and database administrators who were adept at the ins and outs of data. So it was rare for an analyst to know about this new beast called "big data." Whatever the case, these data analytics professionals who got a grip on big data first came to pinpoint its main characteristics, which distinguish it from other, more traditional kinds of data, namely, the so-called 4 V's of big data:

- **Volume** – Big data spans from a very large number of terabytes (TB) and beyond. In fact, a good rule-of-thumb about this characteristic of big data is that if the data is so much that it can't be handled by a single computer, then it's probably big data. That's why big data is usually stored in computer clusters and cloud systems, like Amazon's S3 and Microsoft's Azure, where the total amount of data you can store is virtually limitless (although there are limitations regarding the sizes of the individual uploads, as described in the corresponding webpages, e.g. https://aws.amazon.com/s3/faqs). Naturally, even if the technology to store this data is available, having data at this volume makes analyzing it a challenging task.

- **Velocity** – Big data also travels fast, which is why we often refer to the data we work with as data streams. Naturally, data moving at high bandwidths makes for a completely different set of challenges, which is one of the reasons why big data isn't easy to work with (e.g. fast-changing data makes training of certain models unfeasible, while the data becomes stale quickly, making the constant retraining of the models necessary). Although not all big data is this way, it is often the case that among the data streams that are available in an organization, there are a few that have this attribute.

- **Variety** – Big data is rarely uniform, as it tends to be an aggregate of various data streams that stem from completely different sources. Some of the data is dynamic (e.g. stock prices over time), while other data is fairly static (e.g. the area of a country). Some of the data can come from a database, while the rest of it may be derived from the API of a social medium. Putting all that data together into a format that can be used in a data analytics model can be challenging.

- **Veracity** – Big data is also plagued with the issue of veracity, meaning the reliability of a data stream. This is due to the inherent uncertainty in the measurements involved or the unreliability of the sources (e.g. when conducting a poll for a sensitive topic). Whatever the case, more is not necessarily better, and since the world's data tends to have its issues, handling more of it only increases the chances of it being of questionable veracity, resulting in unreliable or inaccurate predictive models.

Some people talk about additional characteristics (also starting with the letter V, such as variability), to show that big data is an even more unique kind of data. Also, even though it is not considered to be a discernible characteristic of big data specifically, *value* is also important, just like in most other kinds of data. However, value in big data usually becomes apparent only after it is processed through data science.

All of this is not set in stone, since just like data science, big data is an evolving field. IBM has created a great infographic on all this, which can be a good place to dive into this topic further: https://ibm.co/18nYiuo. Also, if you find books and articles stating that there are only three V's of big data, chances are they are outdated, bringing home the point that veracity goes beyond just big data, as it applies to data science books too!

Machine Learning

One of the best ways to work with big data is through a set of advanced analytics methods commonly referred to as Machine Learning (ML). Machine learning is not derived from statistics. In fact, many ML methods take a completely different approach to statistical methods, as they are more data-driven, while statistical methods are generally model-driven. Machine learning methods also tend to be far more scalable, requiring fewer assumptions to be made about the data at hand. This is extremely important when dealing with messy data, the kind of data that is often the norm in data science problems. Even though statistical methods could also work with many of these problems, the results they would yield may not be as crisp and reliable as necessary.

Machine learning is not entirely divorced from the field of statistics. Some ML methods are related to statistical ones, or may use statistical methods on the back-end, as in the case of many regression algorithms, in order to build something with a mathematical foundation that is proven to work effectively. Also, many data science practitioners use both machine learning and statistics, and sometimes combine the results to attain an even better accuracy in their predictions. Keep that in mind when tackling a challenging problem. You don't necessarily have to choose one method or the other. You do need to know the difference between the two frameworks in order to decide how to use each one of them with discernment.

Machine learning is a vast field, and since it has gained popularity in the data analytics community, it has spawned a large variety of methods as well as heuristics. However, you don't need to be an expert in the latest and greatest of ML in order to use this framework. Knowing enough background information can help you develop the intuition required to make good choices about the ML methods to use for a given problem and about the best way to combine the results of some of these methods.

AI – The Scientific Field, Not the Sci-fi Movie!

Machine learning has gained even more popularity due to its long-standing relationship with Artificial Intelligence (AI), an independent field of science that has to do with developing algorithms that emulate sentient beings in their information processing and decision making. A sub-field of computer science, AI is a discipline dedicated to making machines smart so they can be of greater use to us. This includes making them more adept at handling data and using it to make accurate predictions.

Even though a large part of AI research is focused on how to make robots interact with their environment in a sentient way (and without creating a worldwide coop in the process!), AI is also closely linked to data science. In fact, most data scientists rely on it so much that they have a hard time distinguishing it from other frameworks used in data science. When it comes to tackling data analytics problems using AI, we usually make use of *artificial neural networks* (ANNs), particularly large ones. Since the term *large-scale artificial neural networks* doesn't sound appealing nor comprehensive, the term *"deep learning"* was created to describe exactly that. There are several other AI methods that also apply to data science, but this is by far the most popular one; it's versatile and can tackle a variety of data science problems that go beyond predictive analytics (which has been traditionally the key application of ANNs).

The most popular alternative AI techniques that apply to data science are the ones related to fuzzy logic, which has been popular over the years and has found a number of applications in all kinds of machines with limited computational power (for an overview of this framework, check out MathWorks' webpage on the topic at http://bit.ly/2sBVQ3M). However, even though such methods have been applied to data science problems, they are limited in how they handle data, and don't scale as well as ANNs. That's why these fuzzy logic techniques are rarely referred to as AI in a data science setting.

The key benefit of AI in data science is that it is more self-sufficient and relies more on the data than on the person conducting the analysis. The downside of AI is that it makes the whole process of data science superficial and mechanical, not allowing for in-depth analysis of the data. Also, even though AI methods are very good at adapting to the data at hand, they require a very large amount of data, making it impractical in many cases.

The Need for Data Scientists and the Products/Services Provided

Despite the variety of tools and automated processes for processing data available to the world today, there is still a great need for data scientists. There are a number of products and services that we as data scientists offer, even if most of them fall under the umbrella of predictive analytics or data products. Examples are dashboards relaying information about a KPI in real-time, recommendation systems providing useful suggestions for books/videos, and insights geared toward what the demand of product X is going to be or whether patient Y is infected with a disease or not. Also, what we do involves much more than playing around with various models, as is often the case in many Kaggle competitions or textbook problems. So, let's take a closer look at what a data scientist does when working with the given data.

What Does a Data Scientist Actually Do?

A data scientist applies the scientific method on the provided data, to come up with scientifically robust conclusions about it, and to engineer software that makes use of their findings, adding value for whoever is on the receiving end of this whole process, be it a client, a visitor to a website, or the management team.

There are three major activities within the data science process:

- **Data engineering** – This involves a number of tasks closely associated with one another, aiming at getting the data ready for use in the stages that follow. It is not a simple process and difficult to automate. That's why around 80% of our time as data scientists is spent in the stage of data engineering. Luckily, some data is easier to work with than other data, so it's not always that challenging. Also, once you find a way to deploy your creativity in data engineering, it can be a rewarding experience. Regardless, it is a necessary stage of data science, as it is responsible for cleaning up the data, formatting it, and picking the most information-rich parts of it to use later on.

- **Data modeling** – This is probably the most interesting part of the data scientist's work. It involves creating a model or some other system (depending on the application) that takes the data from the previous stage and does something useful with it. This is usually a prediction of sorts, such as "based on the characteristics of data point X, variable Y is going to take the value of 5.2 for that point." The data modeling phase also involves validating the prediction, as well as repeating the process until a satisfactory model is created. It is then applied to data that hasn't been used in the development of this model.

- **Information distillation** – This aspect of the data scientist's work has to do with delivering the insights acquired from the previous stages, communicating them, usually through informative visuals, or in some cases, developing a data product (e.g. an API that takes values of variables related to a client and delivering how likely this person is to be a scammer). Whatever the case, the data scientist ties up any loose ends, writes the necessary reports, and gets ready for the next iteration of the process. This could be with the same data, sometimes enriched with additional data streams. The next iteration may focus on a somewhat different problem, or an improved version of the model.

Naturally, all of these aspects of the data scientist's work are highly sophisticated in practice and are heavily dependent on the problem at hand. The general parts of the data science process, however, remain more or less the same and are useful guidelines to have in mind. We'll go into more detail about all this in the next chapter, where we'll examine the various steps of the data science pipeline and how they relate to each other.

What Does a Data Scientist Not Do?

Equally important to knowing what a data scientist does is knowing what a data scientist doesn't do, since there is a great deal of misconception about the limits of what data science can offer to the world. One of the most obvious but often neglected things that a data scientist cannot do is turn low-veracity data into anything useful, no matter how much of it you give him or how sophisticated a model employed. A data scientist's work may appear as magic to someone who doesn't understand how data science works. However, a data scientist is limited by the data as well as the computing resources available to him. So, even a skilled data scientist won't be able to do much with poor quality data or a miniature of a computer cluster.

Also, a data scientist does not create professional software independently, even if he is able to create an interactive tool that encapsulates the information he has created out of the data. If you expect him to create the next killer app, you may be disappointed. This is why a data scientist usually works closely with software engineers who can build an app that looks good and works well, while also making use of his models on the back-end. In fact, a data scientist tends to have effective collaborations with software developers since they have a common frame of reference (computer programming).

Moreover, a data scientist does not always create his own tools. He may be able to tweak existing data analytics systems and get the most out of them, but if you expect him to create the next state-of-the-art system, you are in for a big disappointment. However, if he is on a team of data scientists who work well together, he may be able to contribute to such a product substantially. After all, most inventions in data science in today's world tend to be the result of cumulative efforts and take place in research centers.

The Ever-growing Need for Data Science Professionals

If so many of us are willing to undergo the time-consuming process of pushing the data science craft to its limits, this is because there is a need for data science and the professionals that make it practical. If today's problems could be solved by business intelligence people or statisticians, they would have. After all, these kinds of professionals are much more affordable to hire, and it's easier to train an information worker in these disciplines. However, if you want to gain something truly valuable from the data that is too elusive to be tackled by conventional data analytics methods, you need to hire a data scientist, preferably someone with the right kind of mindset, one that includes not just technical aptitude, but also creativity, the ability to communicate effectively, and other soft skills not so common among technical professionals.

The need for data science professionals is also due to the fact that most of the data today is highly unstructured and in many cases messy, making it inappropriate for conventional data analytics approaches. Also, the sheer volume of such data being generated has generated the need for more pronounced, scalable predictive analytics. As data science is the best if not the only way to go when it comes to this kind of data analysis, data scientists are an even more valuable resource.

Start-ups tend to be appealing to individuals with some entrepreneurial vocation. However, many of them require a large capital at the beginning, which is hard to find, even if you are business savvy. Nevertheless, data science start-ups don't cost that much to build, as they rely mainly on a good idea and an intelligent implementation of that idea. As for resources, with tech giants like Amazon, Microsoft, and IBM offering their cloud infrastructure equipped with a variety of analytics software at affordable prices, it's feasible to make things happen in this field. Naturally, such companies are bound to focus on spending a large part of their funding to product development, where data scientists play an integral part.

Finally, learning data science has never been as easy a task as it is today. With many books written on it (e.g. the ones from Technics Publications), many quality videos (e.g. the ones on Safari Books Online), and Massive Open Online Courses (MOOC's) (such as edX and Coursera), it is merely a matter of investing time and effort. As for the software required, most of it is open-source, so there is no real obstacle to learning data science today. This whole phenomenon is not random, however, since the increase in available data, the fact that it is messy, and the value this data holds for an organization, indicate that data science can actually be something worthwhile, both for the individual and for the whole. This results in a growing demand for data scientists, which in turn motivates many people who dedicate a lot of time to make this possible. So, take advantage of this privilege, and make the most out of it to jump-start your data science career.

Summary

Data science differs from business intelligence and statistics in these areas:

- peculiarity of the data involved (aka big data)
- messiness of the data
- the use of more advanced data analytics techniques
- the potential of data products
- the inter-disciplinary nature of the field

Big data has four key characteristics:

- **Volume** – it is in very large quantities, unable to be processed by a single computer
- **Velocity** – it is often being generated and transmitted at high speeds
- **Variety** – it is very diverse and comprised of a number of different data streams
- **Veracity** –it is not always high quality, making it sometimes unreliable

Machine learning and AI are two distinct yet important technologies. Machine learning has to do with alternative approaches to data analysis, usually data-driven and employing heuristics and other methods. AI involves various algorithms that enable computers and machines in general to process information to make decisions in a sentient manner.

The three main stages of the data science process are:

1. **Data engineering** – preparing the data so it can be used in the stages that follow
2. **Data modeling** – creating and testing a model that does something useful with the data
3. **Information distillation** – delivering insights from the model, creating visuals, and in some cases, deploying a data product

A data scientist is not a magician, so if the data at hand is of low quality or if there is not enough computing power, it would be next to impossible to produce anything practically useful out of this, no matter how much data is available.

CHAPTER 2

The Data Science Pipeline

Contrary to what many people think, the whole process of turning data into insights and data products is not at all straight-forward. In fact, it's more of an iterative process, with impromptu loops and unexpected situations causing delays and reevaluations of your assumptions. That's why we often talk about the data science pipeline, a complex process comprised of a number of inter-dependent steps, each bringing us closer to the end result, be it a set of insights to hand off to our manager or client, or a data product for our end-user. This whole process is organized in three general stages: data engineering, data modeling, and information distillation (this last one is a term coined by me). Each of these stages includes a number of steps, as you can see in this diagram:

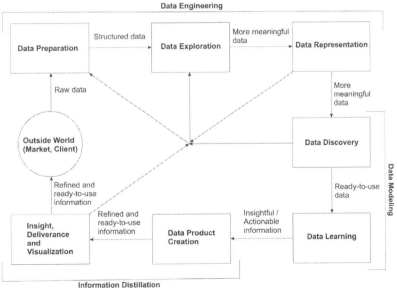

Note that the approach to the data science pipeline described here is just one possible way of viewing it. There are other representations, all of which are equally valid. Also, as the field matures, it may change to adapt to the requirements of the data scientist's role. Keep an open mind when it comes to the data science pipeline, because it is not set in stone.

Now let's look at each one of these steps in more detail.

Data Engineering

Data engineering involves getting your data ready for data analytics work. However, this is not an easy task because data comes in many varieties and degrees of data quality and documentation. In fact, this is the most time-consuming stage of the process, and it's not uncommon for a data scientist to spend 70-80% of their time in this stage.

The main challenge is that most of the data streams involved in a data science project are unstructured or semi-structured data. However, most data analytics models work with structured data (aka datasets), so the raw data streams are practically useless for them. Yet, even if they are structured enough to work, most likely they won't produce sufficiently good results because they are unrefined. The process of refining the data so that they can be of use for modeling is also part of data engineering. In general, this stage involves the following steps:

- Data preparation
- Data exploration
- Data representation

Some people consider data acquisition as part of the process, though nowadays it's so straightforward and automated that it's not worth describing in detail here. Most of the data acquired for a data science project comes from databases (through some query language, like SQL) or from an API.

One thing to note is that even though the aforementioned steps are executed in that order, it is often the case that we need to go back to a previous step and redo it. This iteration in the data science process is quite common in most projects and often involves back-steps from other stages of the pipeline. Let's look at each one of these steps in more detail.

Data Preparation

Data preparation involves cleaning the data and putting it in a data file that can be used for some preliminary analysis. The objective of this step is to get the data ready for exploration, by removing or smoothing out any outliers it may have, normalizing it if necessary, and putting it in a data structure that lends itself for some descriptive analytics. One of the most common such data structures is the data frame, which is the equivalent of a database table.

Data frames have been around for a while and are widely used in data science due to their intuitiveness. It is a very popular data structure in R, Python, Julia, and other programming platforms (even Spark has its variant of data frames). In general, data frames allow for:

- Easy reference of variables by their name
- Easy handling of missing values (usually referred to as NA's or NaN's)
- Variety in the data types stored in them (you can have integers, strings, floats, and other data types in the same data frame, something impossible in matrix and array data structures)

So, loading your data into a data frame is usually a good first step. Of course, depending on the complexity of the problem, you may need to use several data frames and combine them afterwards.

What's important at the data preparation stage is to get it all in one place and put it into a form to play and see what kind of signals are there, if any at all. Whatever the case, you can't be sure about the value of the data without going through the data exploration stage that follows.

Data Exploration

Data exploration is the most interesting part of the pipeline, as it entails playing around with the data without any concrete expectations in order to understand it and find out how to best work with it. This is done primarily by creating a variety of plots. Data exploration is a serious endeavor too, as it involves a lot of quantitative analysis using statistics, particularly descriptive statistics.

Just like in every viable creative endeavor, data exploration involves a combination of intuition and logic; whatever ideas you get by looking at the various plots you create must be analyzed and tested. Several statistical tests come in handy for this, yet data exploration may also involve heuristics designed specifically for this purpose. (More on heuristics in Chapter 11.) If you have heard about stats being the cornerstone of data exploration by some boot-camp instructor, you may want to rethink it. Data science is much more than statistical analysis, even if it involves using statistics to some extent.

At the end of this stage, you should be able to have a sense of what signals the data contains, how strong these signals are, what features are best suited as predictors (if you are dealing with a predictive analytics problem), and what other features you may want to construct using the original feature set. If you have done all this, going to the next step of the data engineering stage will come naturally and without hesitation.

Data Representation

Data representation is about getting the data in the most appropriate data structures (particularly data types) and optimizing the resources used for storing and processing it in the steps that follow. Because even though the data types used to store the variables in the first step of the process may make sense, they may not be the best ones out there for this data. The understanding you have gained from the data exploration step should help you decide on whether the structures should change. Also, you may need to create a few additional features based on the original ones. The data types of these new features' also need to be sorted out at this point.

By the term *features*, we mean data that is in a form that can be used in a model. Features are not the same as variables. In data science, we distinguish between the two based on the processing that has been done on them. Also, a variable may be in the dataset but not be usable in the model as-is.

The transformation from variable to feature can be straight-forward or not, depending on the data. If the data is messy, you may need to work on it before turning the variable into a feature. Whatever the case, after the data representation step, you'll have a set of features at your disposal and have some idea of what each one of them is worth in terms of information content.

Some data science practitioners don't give this step enough attention, because it is often perceived as part of the data preparation or the data exploration phase. However, if you talk to any computer scientist out there, they will tell you that it is very important to choose the right data type for your variables since it can make the difference between having a dataset that's scalable and one that is not. Regardless of the computing power you have access to, you always want to go for a data structure that is more economical in terms of resources, especially if you are planning to populate it with more and more data in the future. This is because such a data structure is more future-proof, while it can also save you a lot of money in cloud resources being utilized. Statisticians may not have to worry about this matter because they usually deal with small or medium data, but in data science, scalability to the big data domain is something that must be kept in mind, even if the data we have at the moment is manageable. Proper data representation can ensure that.

Data Modeling

The data modeling stage is by far the most essential of all three stages of the data science pipeline. This is where the data you have meticulously prepared in the previous stages is turned into something more useful, namely a prediction of or valuable insight. Contrary to what many teach, data modeling is more than just taking functions from a specialized package and feeding it data. It involves much more, probably enough to cover a whole semester's worth of classes.

Everyone can import a package and use it, given they are patient enough to read the corresponding documentation. If you want to do data modeling properly, however, you need to go beyond that. Namely, you need to experiment with a number of models (the more diverse, the better), manage a robust sampling process, and then evaluate each one of these experiments with a few performance metrics.

Afterwards, you may want to combine some of these models, and do another set of experiments. This will not only enable your aggregate model to have a better performance, but also help you delve deeper into the nature of the problem and figure out potential subtleties that you can use to make it better.

Before you even get started with the models, evaluate the features themselves and perhaps do some preliminary analysis on them, followed by some preprocessing. This may involve the generation of meta-features, a process that is common in complex datasets. These two main steps in data modeling are referred to as data learning and data discovery respectively, and are an essential part of insight generation.

Data Discovery

Data discovery is an interesting part of data modeling, as it involves finding patterns and potential insights in the data and building the scaffolds of your model. It is similar to data exploration, but here the focus is on features and how they can be used to build a robust model. Apart from being more targeted, it also entails different techniques. For example, in this step, you may be looking at how certain features correlate to each other, how they would collaborate as a set for predicting a particular target variable, how the graph representation of their information would look, and what insights it can yield.

Forming hypotheses and testing them is something that also plays an important role in this part of the pipeline (it is encountered in the data exploration step too, to some extent). This can only help you identify the signals in the datasets and the features that are of greater value for your model. You also need to get rid of redundant features and perhaps blend the essential features into meta-features (aka synthetic features) for an even better encapsulation of the signals you plan to use. So, in this step, you really go deep into the dataset and mine the insights that are low-hanging fruit, before employing more robust methods in the next step.

Data Learning

Data learning is about creating a robust model based on the discoveries made in the previous step, *as well as testing the model in a reliable manner*. If this sounds like a lot of fun, it's because it is! In fact, most people who take an interest in data science get involved in it because of this step, which is heavily promoted by places like Kaggle (www.kaggle.com), a site hosting various data analytics competitions. Whatever the case, it is definitely the core step of the whole pipeline and deserves a lot of attention from various angles.

The models built in this step are in most cases mappings between the features (inputs) and the target variable (output). This takes the form of a predictive model, or in some cases, some sort of organizing structure (when the target variable is absent). For each general category of models, there are different evaluation criteria that measure the performance of each model. This has to do with how accurate the mapping is and how much time the whole process takes.

Note that the models are usually trained on some part of the dataset and tested on another. This way you can ensure their robustness and general usability (aka generalization). This detail is important, since if it is not taken into account, you risk having models that may seem very accurate but are useless in practice (because they don't generalize). While a big part of this comes from experience, it is equally important (if not more important) to have a solid understanding of how models work and how they are applied, as well as the characteristics of a good model. The best part is that the whole process of acquiring this expertise is fairly quick (you can master it within a year) and very enjoyable, as it involves trying out various options, comparing them, and selecting which one best suits the problem at hand.

Information Distillation

This part of the data science pipeline is about summarizing everything you have done in the previous stages and making it available to your manager or client. This stage is important because of its visibility. Since it's at the end of the pipeline and very close to the deadline of the project, it might be tempting to rush through. Yet, it's imperative to resist this urge and spend the proper time and energy in this stage because it is tied to what the project stakeholders see or experience. Besides, without some solid work in this phase, all the work you've done in the previous parts of the pipeline may not get the visibility they deserve.

Begin by planning for distillation early in the project. For example, keeping a good documentation notebook while you go through the various steps of the pipeline is bound to be useful for this stage, since it's doubtful you will remember all the details of the work you have done in those steps. Also, this kind of documentation will save you time when you prepare your presentations and product documents. In general, information distillation is comprised of two steps: data product creation (whenever there is a data product involved), and insight, deliverance, and visualization.

Data Product Creation

The creation of a data product is often a sophisticated task and isn't mentioned much in other data science pipeline references. This is because in many cases, it has more to do with software engineering or website development. Still, it is an important aspect of data science, as it's the main access point for most people to the data scientists' work.

Data product creation involves an interface (usually accessible through a web browser, as in the case of an API), and an already trained model on the back-end. The user inputs some data through that interface and then waits for a second or so. During that time, the system translates this input into the appropriate features, feeds them to the model, obtains the result of the model, and then outputs it in a form that is easy to understand. During this whole process, the user is completely insulated from all the processes that yield this result.

In some cases, the user can have access to multiple results by paying a license fee to the company that owns the data product. This way, the user can obtain the results of many data points in bulk instead of having to input them one by one.

The creation of data products can be time-consuming and entail some running costs (the cloud servers they live on are not free!). Also, they usually involve the collaborative effort of both data scientists and software engineers; not many projects have the creation of such products as part of their pipeline. However, whenever they have them, this step is usually in the first part of the information distillation stage.

Insight, Deliverance, and Visualization

The deliverance of insights and/or data products and the visualization of the outputs of your analysis are key elements of the data science pipeline and oftentimes the only output of the whole process that is viewed outside the data science team. Still, many data science practitioners don't do this step justice because it is very easy to get absorbed in other, more intriguing parts of the pipeline. The fact that it's the last step of the pipeline doesn't help either.

This part of the information distillation stage generally entails three things:

1. Summary of all the main findings of your analysis into something that is actionable or at least interesting and insightful (hence the first term of this step's name)
2. Deliverance of your work, be it a model or a data product, to the stakeholders of the project
3. Visuals that demonstrate your findings and performance of your model(s)

All of these are important, though what is most important depends on the project and the organization you work for. Regardless, it is best to know that beforehand so you put enough emphasis on that aspect of this phase, ensuring that everyone is as happy about the production cycle's completion as you are.

This step of the data science pipeline is essential even if the rest of the steps can't be completed for one reason or another. Half-baked results are better than no result at all in this case. I don't recommend you leave anything unfinished, but if the time restraints or the data doesn't allow for what you had originally envisioned, it is best to make an effort to present what you've found so that everyone is on the same page with you. If the data is of low veracity for example, and that jeopardized your work, your manager and colleagues need to know. It's not your fault if the data you were given didn't have any strong signals in it.

Putting It All Together

The data science pipeline is a complex beast. Nevertheless, with the right mindset, it is highly useful, providing structure to insight generation and the data product development process. Just like in conventional science, data science's processes are not straight-forward, as every analysis is prone to unforeseen (and many times unforeseeable) situations. As such, being flexible is of paramount importance. That's why we often need to go back to a step we've already spent time on, viewing the problem from different angles until we come up with a model that makes more sense.

If the process seems cyclic in the diagram in the beginning of the chapter, that is because typically it is cyclic in practice. It's not uncommon to have several iterations of the pipeline, especially if the final stage is successful and the stakeholders are satisfied with your outputs. Every iteration is bound to be different. Perhaps you gain access to new data streams, or more data in the existing ones, or maybe you are asked to create a more elaborate model. Whatever the case, iterating over the data science process is far from boring, especially if you treat each iteration as a new beginning!

Summary

The data science pipeline is comprised of three distinct stages:

Data engineering involves refining the data so that it can be easily used in further analysis. It is comprised of three main steps:

1. **Data preparation**: Cleaning the data, normalizing it, and putting it a form that it can be useful for data analysis work
2. **Data exploration**: Playing around with the data to find potential signals and patterns that you can use in your models
3. **Data representation**: Putting the data in the appropriate data structures, saving resources, and optimizing the efficiency of the models that ensue

Data modeling involves creating a series of models that map the data into something of interest (usually a variable you try to predict), as well as evaluating these models through:

- **Data discovery**: Finding useful patterns in the data that can be leveraged in the models as well as optimizing the feature set so that the information in it is expressed more succinctly
- **Data learning**: Developing (training) a series of models, evaluating (testing) them, and selecting those that are better suited for the problem at hand

Information distillation involves summarizing the findings of your analyses and possibly creating a product that makes use of your models using:

- **Data product creation**: Developing an application that uses your model(s) in the back-end
- **Insight, deliverance, and visualization**: Summarizing your findings into actionable insights, delivering them, and creating information-rich visuals

Overall, the pipeline is a highly non-linear process. There are many back-and-forths throughout a data science project, which is why as a data scientist, it's best to be flexible when applying this formula.

CHAPTER 3

Data Science Methodologies

As mentioned in the previous two chapters, data science is diverse in its applications, which is why the pipeline I described is bound to require some adaptation to the problem at hand. This is because data science lends itself to a variety of different situations. Plus the data itself is quite diverse too, making the potential applications different from one another. So using data science, we can engage in a variety of methodologies, such as predictive analytics, recommender systems, automated data exploration (e.g. data mining), graph analytics, natural language processing, and other methodologies.

Predictive Analytics

Predictive analytics is an umbrella of methodologies, all aiming at predicting the value of a certain variable. Predictive analytics methods are the most widely used in data science and also the most researched methods in the field. Their objectives tend to be fairly simple to express mathematically, but achieving a good performance in them is not as straight-forward as you may think. The reason is that in order for a predictive model to work well, it needs to be able to generalize the data it is trained on so that it can grasp the underlying meta-pattern in the data and use that to predict certain things about data it has never encountered before. Therefore, memorizing the patterns in the training data is not only inadequate as an approach, but a terrible idea overall, as this approach is guaranteed to have poor generalization. This condition is usually referred to as over-fitting, and it's a major concern in many data science systems.

Predictive analytics covers a variety of different methodologies which can be grouped into five main categories: classification, regression, time-series analysis, anomaly detection, and text prediction. Let's now look at each one of these predictive analytics methodologies in more detail.

Classification

Whenever we are dealing with a discrete target variable, we have a classification problem. In many cases, the target variable is a binary one (e.g. someone sharing a post in social media or not sharing it), but it can have several different values in the general case (e.g. different types of network attacks). These values are usually referred to as classes, and they can be either numeric or text-based. In some cases, the class variable is transformed into a series of binary variables, one for each class.

Usually we are more interested in predicting one particular value accurately (e.g. fraudulent transactions), rather than all the different values. In the fraudulent transactions case, for example, the other values would be various types of normal transactions, which are expected and common. As such, if we miss a few, it's not a big deal, but missing a few fraudulent transactions may have severe consequences.

The evaluation of a classification system, also known as a classifier, is often measured using a specialized metric called *F1*. If we care about all the different classes equally, then we use a more conventional metric like *accuracy rate* to evaluate our classifier.

There are three different categories of classifiers: inductive/deductive, transductive, and heuristics-based. Inductive/deductive classifiers deal with the creation and application of rules (e.g. decision trees). This excels in cases where the number of features is limited and relatively independent, but fails to handle highly non-linear problems. Transductive classifiers are based on the distances of the unknown data points to the known ones (e.g. K Nearest Neighbor). They are usually good at non-linear problems, are fast, but don't scale very well. Heuristics-based classifiers, which are the most popular one today, make use of various heuristics for creating meta-features which are then used for the classification through some clever aggregation process (e.g. Artificial Neural Networks, or ANNs for short). Although these classifiers tend to perform exceptionally well and are quite scalable, they usually require a lot of data, and their interpretability is questionable.

Regression

Regression deals with problems where the target variable is a continuous one. A common example of this is the number of shares in a post on a social medium. Regression is often linked to classification, since defining a threshold in the target variable of the regression problem can turn it into a binary classification one. Regression hasn't been researched as much as classification, and many of its systems are usually variations of classification ones (e.g. regression trees, which are decision trees that just use a continuous target variable).

The key point of a regression system is that whatever you do, there are always going to be cases where the model is off in relation to the true value of the target variable. The reason is that the model needs to be as simple as possible in order to be robust, and the evaluation functions used tend to focus on the average error (usually the mean squared error).

Regression systems are very useful, yet they are generally a bit left behind compared to other predictive analytics systems because the methods they use for assessing regression features are arcane and sometimes inaccurate (e.g. Pearson Correlation). Contrary to what many people still think, the relationships among variables in the real-world are highly non-linear, so treating them as linear is oversimplifying and distorting them. Also, performing crude transformations on the variables so that these relationships become more or less linear is also a suboptimal approach to the problem. Nevertheless, regression systems are great at doing feature selection on the fly, making the whole process of data modeling faster and easier.

Time-series Analysis

Whenever we have a target variable that changes over time and we need to predict its value in the near future, this involves a time-series analysis (e.g. predicting the value of a stock in the next few days). Naturally, the values we use as features for a problem like that are the previous instances of the target variable, along with other temporal variables. How far back we need to go, however, greatly depends on the problems. Also, the nature of these features, as well as their contributions to the model, are things that need to be determined.

Much like in the case of regression, time-series analysis involves minimizing the error of the target variable, as it also tends to be continuous. The problem in this situation is that a number of predicted data points will have to be used for predicting further into the future, so a small error in the predictions will likely accumulate. This is why problems in this category are more prone to the so-called butterfly effect (see glossary for definition), which is why accurate measurements and predictions are essential for a more robust performance in this kind of system.

Anomaly Detection

The anomaly detection methodology, which is also known as novelty detection, is a very powerful tool for tackling a certain kind of problem that is very hard to solve otherwise. Namely, if you need to identify a certain kind of peculiar case (e.g. fraudulent transactions) in a large number of ordinary ones (in this case, normal transactions). These anomalous cases are usually a problematic situation of a system that, if left unattended, would create a lot of issues in the system and to its end-users. For example, if the data at hand refers to a computer network, an anomalous case could be a hack, blockage, or some system error. Best case scenario, these anomalies are bound to jeopardize the user experience, while they may even bring about security issues to their computers.

Although anomaly detection is in a way a kind of classification, the way it is carried out is not through conventional classification methods. The reason is that conventional classification requires sufficient examples from each of the classes that the predictive analytics system needs to predict. Since this is not possible in some cases due to the anomalies being by definition very rare, classifiers are bound to not learn that particular class properly, making predictions of it inaccurate.

A special kind of anomaly detection is outlier prediction for a single variable. Although this scenario is fairly basic, since it is usually the case that the outliers can be pinpointed very accurately, often without any calculations at all, that's not a trivial problem either. As the dimensionality increases, it becomes more and more challenging, since the statistical methods which have been used traditionally in figuring out extreme cases fail to predict anomalies accurately. That's why most modern anomaly detection techniques rely primarily on machine learning, or non-parametric data analytics, such as kernel methods.

Anomaly detection is important in various domains, such as cybersecurity. Needless to say, even if the majority of cases are benign, the few malicious ones can be catastrophic, making their prediction a highly valuable feat that would be practically impossible without anomaly detection.

Text Prediction

This predictive analytics methodology, text prediction, has to do with predicting the word or phrase that comes next in a textual data stream (e.g. when typing a query in the search bar of a search engine). Although it may not seem like a difficult problem, it is. It requires a lot of data in order to build a robust text predictor. For the system to work properly and in real-time, as is usually the case, it has to calculate loads of conditional probabilities on the fly. This is so it can pick the most probable word among the thousands of possible words in a given language, to follow the stream of words it has at its disposal. It is a bit like time-series analysis, though in this case, the target variable is discrete and of a different type (i.e. not numeric).

Text prediction has many applications in the mobile world, especially related to smartphones, as it lends itself for facilitating text input. Also, a version of it is used in text editors like Notepad++ for inputting large variable names, for example. In this kind of application, its scope is far more limited, so it's a fairly easy scenario, but when dealing with the whole of a language's vocabulary, a more robust predictive system is required.

Recommender Systems

Also known as recommendation systems, this is probably one of the most widely known applications of data science, as it is quite ubiquitous. From online stores to the Internet Movie Database (IMDb), various sites make use of a recommender system. Basically, a recommender system takes a series of entities (e.g. consumer products), which are often referred to as *items*, and which are associated with another list of entities (e.g. customers), often referred to as *users*. It then tries to figure out what an existing member of the latter list will be interested in from all the members of the former list. This may seem straight-forward, but considering the vast amount of combinations and the fact that the overlap between two users is bound to be small, this makes for a challenging problem.

The matrix that encapsulates all the information on the relationship between the items and the users is usually referred to as the *utility matrix*, and it is key in all recommender systems. However, as these relationships tend to be very specialized, this matrix is usually very sparse and very large. This is why it is usually represented as a sparse matrix type when doing data analytics work on it.

In order to make use of the data in the utility matrix, there have been several methods developed that facilitate this recommendation process to make it fairly easy and quite scalable. These methods aim to fill in the blanks in the utility matrix and give us hints about potential relationships between users and items not yet manifested in real life. Let's take a look at the most important categories, namely collaborative filtering and content-based systems, both of which play an important role in recommender systems. If we are dealing with a case where various users rate a bunch of items in an e-commerce store, the collaborative filtering method deals with the user ratings, while the content-based approach focuses on using features of items to calculate their similarity. On top of all that, there is a strictly analytical approach called Non-negative Matrix Factorization, which is also used in practice. Let's look at each one of these methods in more detail.

Content-based Systems

Content-based systems take a more traditional approach to recommendations. They look at how we can create features based on the items and use them as a proxy for finding similar items to recommend. As a first step, this method attempts to formulate a profile for each item. You can think of this as an abstraction of the item that is common among other items which share certain characteristics. In the case of movies, for example, these can be the genre, the director, the production company, the actors, and even the time it was first released.

Once you have decided on which features to use for the item profile, you can re-factor all the available data so that it takes the form of a feature set. These features can be binary ones, denoting the presence or absence of something. This is common in some applications, such as cases where the items are documents or web pages. The features are then used for assessing similarities using metrics such as the inverted *Jaccard distance* and *cosine distance*. The specific metric you use greatly depends on the application at hand and the dimensionality of the feature set. Also, these feature sets lend themselves to predictive analytics methods (particularly classification), so using the latter as part of a recommender system is also an effective option.

Collaborative Filtering

The collaborative filtering method of recommendation has been around the longest and involves finding similarities between the user ratings for two items, thereby finding similar users and applying transductive reasoning for finding the more relevant items to recommend.

As for measuring the similarity among the users, there are various methods for that. Like in the content-based recommender systems, the most common ones here are the inverted Jaccard distance and cosine distance, though the process of collaborative filtering also involves certain other processes. For example, rounding the data and performing some kind of normalization are popular.

Collaborative filtering also entails some clustering methods. This shouldn't come as a shock, considering that clustering is about finding similar data points and putting them into groups. The recommendation problem is a classic-use case for this methodology. Though, one thing to keep in mind is that the number of clusters is best to remain large, at least at first, for the clusters to be more meaningful.

Beyond these methods of collaborative filtering, there is also the more analytical approach of UV decomposition, where the utility matrix is split (decomposed) into two other matrices. This is a computationally expensive process, but solves the problem very efficiently. We'll look into a popular UV decomposition method in the next paragraph.

Non-negative Matrix Factorization (NMF or NNMF)

Although this is technically a collaborative filtering method, its robustness and popularity render it a method worthy of its own section in this book. As the name suggests, it involves breaking a matrix into two other matrices that when multiplied together, yield the original matrix. Also, the values of these new matrices are either zero or positive, hence the "non-negative" part.

Factorizing a matrix can be modeled as an optimization problem, where the fitness function is the squared error. However elegant as it is, such a process is prone to over-fitting. One very robust remedy to this is a process called *regularization* (which is also used in regression problems extensively). This is incorporated in the NMF algorithm, something that contributes to the effectiveness of this technique. The two matrices that this process yields, P and Q, are often referred to as the *features matrix* and the *weights matrix* respectively. Each row in P represents the strength of the connections between the user and the features, while every row in Q denotes the strength of the connections between an item and the features.

The features in P are the latent features that emerge from this analysis, which may have real-world expressions (e.g. a film's genre, in the case of a movie recommender system). In general, there are fewer features than items, otherwise the system would be impractical.

Automated Data Exploration Methods

This group of data science methods involves an automated approach to data exploration. Generally, they are fast, insightful, and oftentimes useful for the problems they are opting to solve. Its main method is data mining, but there are also other ones like association rules and clustering. Let's look at each one of the main methods of this group in more detail.

Data Mining

Data mining has been around even before data science was an independent discipline. Now it can be considered as part of it, since it is generally an automated form of data exploration. The focus of data mining is finding patterns in the data without the use of a specific model. In fact, it rarely involves the development of any models, as it is mainly interested in finding relationships among the different variables of the dataset. Oftentimes, there isn't even a target variable involved in the problems that it's trying to solve. So, for problems like that, data mining is an excellent approach. Afterwards, you can shift to different methodologies to address specific questions that involve a target variable.

Data mining has fallen out of fashion in the past years, as it was geared toward data analysts who didn't have the programming expertise and in-depth understanding of data analytics to go beyond the analysis that data mining yields. As such, it is not considered a groundbreaking field any more, although it is a useful methodology to know, particularly if you are dealing with huge sparse datasets, especially containing text.

Association Rules

Although this is technically part of data mining, it is worth describing a bit further on its own, as its results are very useful. Association rules are usually related to a particular application: shopping carts. In essence, they involve insights derived from the creation of rules about what other products people buy when products A and B are in their shopping carts.

Rules may vary in applicability and reliability. These two attributes are the key characteristics of a rule and are referred to as support and confidence respectively once they are quantified as metrics. Usually these metrics take the form of a percentage. The higher they are, the more valuable the rules are. So, data exploration through finding/creating association rules is the process of pinpointing the most valuable such rules based on a given dataset. The number of rules and the thresholds of support and confidence tend to be the parameters of this process.

You can find an example at Professor Zdravko Markov's webpage at the Central Connecticut State University website: http://bit.ly/2m391bh.

Clustering

Clustering is a popular data exploration method that often goes beyond the data exploration part of the pipeline. Although most of the clustering methods out there are still rudimentary and require some parameter tuning, as a methodology, clustering is highly valuable and insightful. Usually categorized as an unsupervised learning method (since it doesn't require any labeled data), it finds groups of data points that are most similar, while at the same time most dissimilar to the data points of the other groups. The rationale of this methodology is finding interesting patterns in a dataset, if the data you have is quantitative. (If you have binary variables too, that would also work as long as they are not *all* binary variables.) These patterns take the form of labels, which can be used to provide more structure to your dataset.

An important thing to keep in mind when using this method is to always have your data normalized, preferably to [0, 1] or to (0, 1), if you plan to include binary variables. Also, it is important to pick the right distance function (the default is Euclidean, but Manhattan distance is also useful in certain problems), since different distance functions yield different results. If the number of variables is high, you may want to reduce it before applying clustering to your data. This is because high dimensionality translates to a very sparse data space (making it harder to identify the signal in the dataset), while most distance metrics fail to capture the differences/similarities of the various data points. Finally, in some cases, like when using a variant of the k-means algorithm, you will need to provide the number of clusters (usually referred to as k), since it is an essential parameter of the algorithm.

Graph Analytics

Graph analytics makes use of a fairly intuitive representation of the data, primarily focusing on the relationships among the various data points (or features/classes, in some cases). Although this methodology's name hints towards a visual approach to data analytics, it is not bound by that aspect of it. In fact, graph analytics involves a lot of calculations which are abstract in nature, much like traditional computer science. The key facets of this methodology are that graphs are in a different domain, beyond the n-dimensional space of conventional data analytics, and that graphs are made useful through the various algorithms that make the innate information in these graphs available to the data scientists.

In general, a graph is comprised of three things:

- **Nodes** (aka vertices): the entities that are of primary importance in the dataset

- **Arcs** (aka edges): the connections among these entities, represented as lines
- **Weights**: the values corresponding to the strength of these connections

Dimensionless Space

Graphs live in an abstract plane where all the conventional dimensions are absent. Therefore, they are not prone to the limitations of the conventional space which most datasets inhabit. This frees graphs from issues like the curse of dimensionality or the signal being diluted by useless features. Also, because graphs can be easily viewed on a screen or a print-out, they lend themselves to easy data visualization.

In order to get data into graph form, you need to define a similarity/dissimilarity metric, or a relationship that is meaningful in the data at hand. Once you do that, you can model the data as follows: Nodes are the data points, features, clusters, or any other entities you find most important; Arcs are the relationships identified; Weights are the values of the similarities/ dissimilarities calculated for these relationships.

After you have identified the architecture of the graph, you can create a list of all the nodes, their connections, and their weights, or put all this information in a large, usually sparse, matrix. The latter is typically referred to as the connectivity matrix and is very important in many algorithms that run on graphs. Let's look at some of those algorithms and how they can be of use to your data science projects.

Graph Algorithms

These are specialized algorithms, designed for graph-based data, and are adept at providing insights related to the relationship dynamics and the connectivity of the entities involved in the graphs they are applied to. Graph algorithms are not always relevant to data science, but it's good to know them nevertheless, as they enable you to comprehend the dynamics of graph theory and how the flow of information is mirrored in the graph architecture. This makes them useful in data exploration.

The graph algorithms that are most commonly used are the following:

- **Calculating graph characteristics** (e.g. centrality, order, power, and eccentricity) – These pertain to certain aspects of the graphs, the equivalent of descriptive statistics in a tabular dataset.

- **Creating the Minimum Spanning Tree of a graph** (Prim's and Kruskal's algorithms) – These are the graphs connecting all the nodes in the smallest overall weight. They are the skeleton of the graph.

- **Finding the shortest path between two nodes** (Dijkstra's and Floyd's algorithms) – These are the core algorithms for all navigation systems, particularly those that are GPS-based.

- **Finding connected components** – These are "islands" of connectivity in a graph and are particularly useful in sparse graphs. Finding them can yield useful insights.

- **Finding cliques** (highly connected sub-graphs) – Much like connected components, cliques are high-density areas of connectivity. The only difference is that the nodes of a clique can be connected to other nodes outside the clique.

- **Finding a Maximal Independent Set** (aka MIS; Luby's algorithm) – An independent set in a graph is a set of nodes where any pair within it is not directly connected. A maximal independent set is an independent set S, where if we were to add any other node to S, the independence would no longer hold properly. Finding sets like this can be useful in understanding a graph's entities.

- **Finding Single-Source Shortest Paths** (Johnson's algorithm) – This is very much like finding shortest paths, but it applies on sparse graphs only.

- **Calculating the PageRank value of a node** (any modern search engine's core algorithm) – This is a clever way of figuring out the importance of a node in a graph based on how many nodes point toward it. It applies only to a certain kind of graph, where the relationship's direction is modeled (also known as directed graphs). This is essential for ranking the nodes in a graph.

- **Clustering nodes in a graph** – This is the equivalent of conventional clustering, but applied to graph-based data. It yields subsets of the original graph that are more closely connected and is essential for understanding the nature of the different kinds of entities in the graph and how they are interrelated.

Although this list is not exhaustive, it is an excellent place to start in traversing the knowledge graph of graph analytics tools.

Other Graph-related Topics

Apart from graph modeling and graph processing (through the various algorithms out there), there are certain other things that should be taken into account when using graphs in data science projects.

Storing graphs, for example, is much different than storing conventional datasets and requires some attention. Ideally, your graph could be stored in a single file (given it's compact enough) as a graph object. However, if your graph contains an excessive amount of data, it may need to be stored in a distributed format. Whatever the case, if you are planning to do a lot of work with graphs, it would make sense to use a graph database system, such as Neo4j. This kind of software will not only store your graph efficiently, but also query it and help you enrich it through its dedicated language (in the case of Neo4j, it is Cypher, and its scripts have the .cql extension). More often than not, these graph programs will have APIs for certain programming languages, so you won't need to do everything through their native scripts.

Graphs are also dynamic. As such, they often require special treatment. For example, algorithms for evolving graphs are great for this kind of situation and are popular in the corresponding domains (e.g. social media). Evolving graphs have a temporal component. As a result, the analysis you perform on them is different than that of conventional (static) graphs.

Clearly, not every problem lends itself to a graph-based solution. While graph analysis is attractive and very appealing to anyone who understands the underlying theory, it doesn't mean that it's a panacea. If your problem involves relationships of entities and how they change over time, then graph analysis is the best way to go for your data science project.

Natural Language Processing (NLP)

Natural language processing is a fascinating part of data science that involves making sense out of text and figuring out certain characteristics of the information in it, such as its sentiment polarity, its complexity, and the themes or topics it entails. Although there are a lot of data science professionals involved in this part of data science doing all sorts of interesting things, the field remains in its infancy, as most of them just do one or more of the following NLP tasks: sentiment analysis, topic extraction, and text summarization. We have yet to see a system in NLP that actually understands what text it is being fed and does something intelligent with it.

Sentiment Analysis

Sentiment analysis is one of the most popular NLP methods. It involves finding out whether a piece of text has a positive or negative flavor (although in certain cases a neutral flavor may also be an option, depending on the application). The idea is to identify if a piece of text is polarized emotionally, and to gauge the pulse of public opinion on a topic (in the case of multiple texts, usually stemming from social media). However, sentiment analysis lends itself to the analysis of internal documents in an organization, such as call logs.

There are several ways to accomplish sentiment analysis; all of them involve creating a set of features which are then fed into a binary classifier (oftentimes a simple logistic regression system). The effectiveness of this method lies in the selection of the most powerful features that most effectively encapsulate the information in the text. The presence of certain key words that are known to be either positive or negative can be good candidates for such features. Usually the selection of the words or phrases that are then used for these features is an automated process. The whole process can also be modeled as a regression problem, yielding a flavor score as an output, ranging between 0.0 (negative sentiment) and 1.0 (positive sentiment).

Sentiment analysis, even if it is not very accurate, is a very useful application, especially when it comes to analyzing text feeds from social media in order to gauge how people feel about a certain topic (e.g. the political situation, a certain event, or even a particular person). An example of this is the sentiment analysis of a particular commercial product, using its reviews from various sources. The information stemming from the sentiment analysis of this data stream could help a company figure out the optimum marketing strategy for that product, as well as optimize the way to engage with its customers.

Don't underestimate the value of this method because of its simplicity. Sentiment analysis is so insightful that there are companies out there that are built solely around this service.

Topic Extraction/Modeling

Topic extraction (aka topic modeling) entail the discovery of the most distinct groups of topics in a set of documents based on a statistical analysis of the key terms featured. This analysis is usually based on some frequency model, which basically translates to the number of occurrences of the terms in the documents. Whatever the case, it works well and always provides a set of topics, along with a view of how the given documents relate to these topics. The most commonly used algorithm for this is the *Latent Dirichlet Allocation (LDA)*, although there are others too. LDA is quite popular because of its ability to handle whole word phrases, rather than individual words only.

Naturally, regardless of the algorithm you use for finding these topics, certain words are usually excluded from the text because they don't add much value to the documents. These are usually very common words (e.g. the, and, a, by), which are often referred to as *stopwords*. Also, they can be other words, or even whole phrases, that are specific to the documents analyzed (e.g. USA, country, United States, economy, senator, if the document corpus is comprised of talks by US politicians, for example).

Topic extraction/modeling is essential for organizing large collections of text that are in the form of individual documents. These can be articles, website content, or even whole books. This NLP method enables you to figure out what these documents are about without having to parse them yourself so that you can then analyze the document corpus more effectively and efficiently. If you don't want to code this yourself, there is a freely available tool developed by Stanford University that you can use: http://stanford.io/2lYbtUv.

Text Summarization

As its name suggests, this method of NLP has to do with encapsulating the key ideas in a document in a new document that is shorter, yet still in a comprehensive text form. Coupled with this is the process of named entity recognition, which has to do with identifying certain entities (e.g. people involved, their titles, time, and location) and delivering all the key information related to them (e.g. what kind of event took place). Some people consider sentiment analysis as part of text summarization, although I would rather keep it separate here, as it has grown to be a fairly independent field as of late.

There are several methods for text summarization, all of which fall into one of two categories: supervised and unsupervised. Just like the corresponding machine learning method categories, these ones share the same philosophy: if there is labeled data and it's leveraged in the method, it is supervised. Otherwise, it is unsupervised.

Some of the major supervised methods of text summarization are grouped as follows:

- **Statistical**: Conditional Random Field, KEA, KEA++ (Naive Bayes)

- **Conventional ML**: Turney (SVM), GenEx (Decision Tree), KPSpotter (Information Gain coupled with a combination of other NLP techniques)
- **AI related**: Artificial Neural Networks

In the unsupervised methods category, some of the methods that exist are:

- **Statistical**: Frequency analysis, TF-IDF, BM25, POS-tags
- **Other**: TextRank, GraphRank, RAKE

Other NLP Methods

Beyond these methods in NLP, there are a few other NLP methods that deserve your attention if you are to employ NLP in your projects. For example, the breakdown of a text into its parts-of-speech (POS) structure is also popular and is usually carried out with a package like NLTK or spaCy, in Python.

Other methods of NLP may focus more on the complexity of the text, using custom algorithms that analyze the breadth of the vocabulary used, the length of each sentence, and other similar factors. This is particularly useful when it is taken to the next level to look into more subtle things, like writing style (expressed in different features, such as text entropy and sentence structure). This can be used to check if two documents are written by the same person (plagiarism detection).

Finally, there are other NLP methods that are used in conjunction with graph analysis or other data science methodologies. These may involve information retrieval topics such as relevance of a document to a given phrase (query), using methods like TF-IDF (term frequency-inverse document frequency), a heuristic for assessing how important a particular term is in a document in relation to other terms across a set of documents.

All of these methods merely scratch the surface of what is possible in the NLP field. For example, NLP also includes methods for generating text, figuring out the text's parts-of-speech, and many more.

Other Methodologies

Beyond the aforementioned methodologies that are used in data science, there are other ones as well, most of which have come about relatively recently. They are mostly AI-related, and as this field is on the rise, you can expect to see more of these cropping up in the years to come. Let's look at some of them now that are popular among data scientists.

Chatbots

Chatbots are NLP systems that are interactive, dwell in the cloud, and are usually associated with a particular set of real-world tasks. They serve as virtual assistants of sorts, always there to help out with queries and carrying out relatively simple tasks. The function of a chatbot entails the following processes (in that order), all of which are data-science related to some extent:

- **Understanding what the user types** (or in some cases, speaks) – This employs an NLP system that analyzes the language, identifies key words and key phrases, and isolates them
- **If the input is audio and the system is uncertain** (or if its settings demand it to do so) – In this case, a confirmation response is given, where the system repeats what the user has said to ensure that it has understood it properly
- **Information retrieval/task completion** – This involves carrying out the task that relates to the user's request, be it a simple informational one or a more executive one
- **Final response** – The chatbot yields the information retrieved or a brief report regarding the task performed to the user

Chatbots are great for customer service, general assistance with the visitors of a complex website, or even with day-to-day tasks, as in the case of Amazon Echo. There are several open-source systems, and they are often domain-specific. A key benefit of chatbots is that everything they do is logged. If the systems in the back-end are properly designed, a chatbot can use this data to improve itself, making the communication with the user smoother and more reliable over time.

Although the technology is still fairly new and has plenty of room for improvement, it is gaining ground rapidly. As NLP methods continue to enhance, chatbots are bound to be much more useful in the future. If you are interested in NLP, this is definitely an area worth monitoring closely.

Artificial Creativity

This niche methodology of data science is really an AI technology and involves the use of sophisticated systems, usually ANN-based, that mimic certain styles to create new data either from scratch or using preexisting material (e.g. a photograph, in the case of digital painting). However, artificial creativity is not only related to the arts (e.g. music, painting, and poetry). It covers other, more practical areas of application too, such as document writing (e.g. in the case of news articles) and product design. Automated software testing is also something that's gained traction over the past few years (computer-generated tests tend to be broader and therefore the testing that ensues is more robust).

The application where artificial creativity truly shines, however, at least when it comes to data science, is coming up with novel solutions to problems. Artificial creativity is of paramount importance when it comes to feature engineering (e.g. through Deep Learning systems as well as Genetic Programming). If you are interested in coming up with novel ways to expand your feature set, this is a field worth exploring. The catch is that you need to have a lot of (labeled) data in order to do this properly; otherwise the new feature set is bound to be subject to over-fitting.

Other AI-based Methods

Beyond chatbots and artificial creativity, there are several other AI-based methodologies that are used in data science, directly or indirectly. Let's take a brief look at some of them that have been around long enough to demonstrate their timelessness and viability in this ever-changing field.

First and foremost, optimization is one of the methods that is essential for any data-science related problem, and it is used under the hood in many of the aforementioned methodologies. It involves finding the best (or one of the best) set of parameter values of a function, in order to make its output maximum or minimum. However, it can be necessary to apply it on its own for finding the best possible solution to a well-defined problem, under certain restrictions, especially in cases where there are several variables involved and the problem cannot be solved analytically. Yet even in cases where there is an analytic solution possible, we resort to optimization in order to obtain a solution faster, regardless of if that solution is not the absolute best one. This is because an analytical solution is bound to take much more time and computational resources to calculate, while this extra cost is not always justified, since a near-optimum solution is often good enough for all practical purposes.

A few AI methods for optimization that have been proven to be both robust and versatile are Genetic Algorithms, Particle Swarm Optimization (and its many variants), and Simulated Annealing. Which one is best depends on the application and the data at hand, so I recommend that you learn to use all of them, even if you don't know the specifics of the algorithms involved in great detail.

AI-based reasoning is another AI methodology that is very popular among theoretical scientists. It involves getting the computer to perform logical operations in logical statements. These are often used to conduct proofs of theorems, which augment the existing scientific knowledge by facilitating research (particularly in Mathematics). They can also be useful for data science projects, particularly if you make use of a rule-based system. This kind of artificial reasoning can be useful for conveying insights as well as handling high-level administration of data analytics systems in a manner that is easy to understand and communicate to the stakeholders of a project.

Fuzzy logic is a classic AI methodology that is similar to reasoning, but involves a different framework for modeling data (see http://bit.ly/2sBVQ3M for an overview of the topic). Also, contrary to all statistical approaches which are probabilistic in nature, fuzzy logic is possibilistic and involves levels of membership to particular states rather than chance. Since variable states are not clear-cut in fuzzy logic, there is a sense of realism in how it treats its entities, as we as human beings tend not to see things in black-and-white for everyday things. Nevertheless, fuzzy logic operators resemble closely the operators of conventional logic, though they employ different approaches for implementing them. No matter, the end result is always crisp, and the whole process of getting there is quite comprehensive, making this framework a very practical and easy-to-use tool.

The main limitations of fuzzy logic are that it ceases to be intuitive when the number of variables increases, and it takes a lot of work to set up the membership functions, often requiring input from domain experts. Nevertheless, it is a useful methodology to have in mind as it is easy to apply to existing data science systems, such as classifiers, improving their performance.

Summary

Data science involves a variety of different methodologies dealing with a number of different applications. These can be grouped into the following general categories:

Predictive analytics – These systems involve predicting the value of a variable given a set of data (aka training set):

- Classification – handles cases where the target variable is discrete
- Regression – deals with cases where the target variable is continuous
- Time-series analysis – focuses on cases where the target variable changes over time
- Anomaly detection – identifies peculiar cases that, although very rare, are important to find, as they usually represent problematic situations
- Text prediction – relates to scenarios where the data involved is text

Recommender systems – These systems involve finding something relevant (similar) to recommend to a user based on that user's history and the histories of similar users, the most important of which are:

- Content-based Systems – focuses on the use of features of items to determine their similarity
- Collaborative Filters – focuses on the similarity of user ratings
- Non-negative Matrix Factorization (NMF) – substitutes the utility matrix with two other matrices whose product approximates the original matrix

Automated data exploration – These are various techniques that are useful for finding relationships among the variables, as well as anything else that can be used to understand the patterns in the dataset:

- Data mining – Usually model-free methods for data analytics, it opts to derive patterns across different types of data
- Association rules – Usually application-specific, they aim to show how the presence of certain characteristics in a data point denote the presence or absence of a high-level phenomenon of interest
- Clustering – This has to do with finding groups in the dataset that correspond to data points similar to one another and also different from data points of other groups

Graph analysis – This methodology has to do with representing data in a dimensionless space, modeling the relationships among all of its entities, calculating certain statistics of the graph that ensues, and deriving insights from its dynamics through various algorithms. Graphs are comprised of four main components:

- Nodes – the entities of the data that we wish to examine, usually represented by compact circles
- Arcs – the relationships among the entities, represented by straight or curved lines connecting the nodes
- Weights – the number values corresponding to these relationships
- Connectivity matrix – a matrix summarizing all the above information (when the graph is sparse, this is a sparse matrix)

Natural Language Processing (NLP) – This approach to data science involves the analysis of text data to derive insights related to its content. NLP has a variety of methods attached to it, such as:

- Sentiment analysis – finding out if the overall sentiment of a piece of text is positive or negative (or in some cases, neutral)
- Topic extraction – finding the most distinct groups of topics, based on a frequency analysis of the key terms featured in a set of documents
- Text summarization – capturing the key ideas in a document and creating a new document that is shorter but retains these ideas in a comprehensive text form

Other methodologies – Involve mainly modern systems, such as:

- Chatbots – involves somewhat intelligent virtual assistants that perform queries or simple tasks for us, making use of NLP and other technologies
- Artificial Creativity – has to do with finding novel ways to perform something, be it in the arts domain or in more practical endeavors, such as document writing, product design, or creating artificial features
- Other AI-based methodologies – optimization, AI-based reasoning, fuzzy logic, and other AI frameworks that are useful and oftentimes essential in data science

CHAPTER 4

The Data Scientist's Toolbox

A lot has been said about what a data scientist needs to know in terms of data tools and software. People's views oscillate between the two extremes of either needing at least one virtual machine on the cloud, equipped with everything the "experts" think we need, and not needing anything at all apart from a programming language (usually Python) and a personal computer. Unfortunately, things are not so simple. A data scientist's toolbox includes many things, ranging from specialized software, to programming languages, to data science packages for these languages. What is essential for you depends on a) how much money you are willing to spend, and b) the sophistication of the problem you are trying to solve. So, instead of giving you a recipe to follow, I am going to provide you with all the various options and leave the decision of what best suits your needs to the only person capable of it: you.

Database Platforms

The data needs to live somewhere, and chances are that it is not always in neat .csv files like the ones you see in Kaggle (a machine learning competition site). More often than not, the data you use dwells in a database. Whatever the case, even if it is not in a database originally, you may want to put it in one during the data engineering phase for easier handling, since it is not uncommon for the same data to be used in different data science projects. If the data is all over the place, you may want to tidy it up and put it in a database where you can easily access it, to create the datasets you will use in your project(s).

Databases come in all shapes and forms these days. However, they are generally in one of three broad categories: SQL-based, NoSQL, and graph-based.

SQL-based Databases

SQL-based databases are the ones that make use of some variant of the Structured Query Language (SQL), a fairly basic language that is designed to interact with conventional databases and, most commonly, fire queries at them. As the name suggests, these databases are structured, meaning that they have a fixed set of fields in each table, and all their content is organized in tables which are connected through special fields, called keys. Also, SQL-based databases are generally handled with a database management system (DBMS), although there are APIs for them in various programming languages too.

This sort of database is useful for storing data that comes from web forms, software, and spreadsheets. They are great for conventional uses of data storage and retrieval, which is why they are popular in companies. Even if they are not the best for data science applications, they are bound to be something you will encounter, at least for some of the data streams you'll use in your projects.

This tutorial on TutorialsPoint is a great place to start if you need to refresh your SQL knowledge: http://bit.ly/2ntQJEq. Keep in mind that the vanilla flavor of SQL may not be 100% compatible with other SQL-based databases, such as MySQL (which is heavily used in web applications).

NoSQL Databases

NoSQL databases are databases that allow the data to be unstructured, although it could be structured as well (the "No" part of their name stands for "not only," and is probably the most confusing naming convention you will encounter in data science). Because of their flexibility and high speed, NoSQL databases are the norm in data science, as no one in their right mind stores big data in conventional databases. Nevertheless, SQL is still a useful language to know even in this kind of database, since the query language that NoSQL databases use is generally similar to SQL.

NoSQL databases are usually handled through APIs, although DBMSs are also an option. The most popular such databases are:

- Cassandra
- CouchDB
- DocumentDB
- HBase
- Hive
- MariaDB
- MongoDB
- Redis

The key advantages of NoSQL databases are elastic scaling and flexibility, as well as low cost (mainly due to the fact that a NoSQL database doesn't rely on a DBMS). Also, HBase and Hive are part of the Hadoop ecosystem, which will be discussed shortly.

If you want to learn about a NoSQL database, you can either check out a tutorial (http://bit.ly/2nxFXtL) or download the database software and play around with it, using the documentation (or a specialized book) as a guide. Also, be sure to check out the corresponding packages in the programming language you use, since it is much more convenient to access the NoSQL database this way.

Graph-based Databases

Graph databases are somewhat different than the other ones, as they focus on creating, storing, querying, and processing graphs. However, several of the modern database platforms are multipurpose, so they handle all kinds of objects, including graphs.

Here are five of the most powerful databases that can handle graphs (some of them exclusively):

- **Neo4j** – native graph database, specializing in this particular kind of data structure
- **AllegroGraph** – high-performance graph database
- **Teradata Aster** – multipurpose high-performance database
- **ArangoDB** – multipurpose distributed database
- **Graphbase** – distributed and resource-cheap database specializing in very large graphs

Although most of these databases are similar, Neo4j stands out, as it is one of the most mature ones in this domain. Also, it is highly different from the multipurpose ones; it is built around graphs, rather than just to accommodate them. You can learn more about it either at its site's Getting Started page (http://bit.ly/2maQfmq) or at its Tutorials Point section (http://bit.ly/2nzQgNU).

Programming Languages for Data Science

Data science is inherently different than conventional data analytics approaches, and one of the key differentiating factors is programming. This is the process of creating a custom program that runs on a computer or a cloud server and processes data to provide an output related to this data, using a specialized coding language.

Excel scripting is not programming, just as creating an automated process in SAS doesn't qualify. Programming is a separate discipline that is not rocket science, though it is not simple either. Of course, there are programming languages that are fairly simple, like Scratch (a game-focused language ideal for kids), but these are designed for very specialized applications and do not lend themselves for real-world scenarios. In data science, we have a set of programming languages that, because of their ease of use and variety of packages (programming libraries), lend themselves to the various methodologies we examined in the previous chapter. The most important of these languages are Julia, Python, R, and Scala.

Julia

Julia is probably the best data science language out there, partly because it is super-fast, and partly because it is very easy to prototype in. Also, whatever code you write in Julia is going to be as fast as the code you can find in its data science packages. What's more, the combination of these features allows it to be the production language for your code, so you won't need to translate everything into C++ or Java in order to deploy it. Julia was developed at MIT and has gained popularity all over the world since then through conferences (JuliaCon) and meet-ups.

This growing user-community allows it to provide some support to new users, making it easier for people to learn it. Also, as it is designed with the latest programming language standards, it is more future-proof than most other languages out there. However, due to its young age, it does not have all the data science libraries of other, more established languages, and there are lots of changes from one release to the next. Another thing to note, which is a more neutral characteristic of Julia, is that it is primarily a functional language. This is a different programming paradigm than the object-oriented languages that dominate the programming world these days, and which focus on objects and classes, rather than pieces of code performing certain tasks. Yet, Julia has a lot of elements of that paradigm too.

Overall, Julia is a great multipurpose language that lends itself to data science. Its newness should not deter you from using it in your data science projects. In fact, this newness can be a good thing. You'd be one of the early adopters of a language which is gaining popularity quickly in both industry and academia. This way, in a few years, when more companies are aware of this language's merits and have it as a requirement for their recruits, you'll be among the most experienced candidates.

Python

Python is what Julia would look like if it were developed 20 years earlier. An easy, object-oriented language, it has been used extensively for all kinds of scripts (some people classify it as a scripting language). Over the past few years, it has become popular in the data science community, particularly version 2.7, as that fork of it has the majority of the data science packages of the language.

Python's high-level style makes it easy to learn and debug, yet it is fairly slow, which is why all code developed in this language is usually translated into a low-level language in order to gain performance. Its large set of libraries for all kinds of data science methods enable its users to utilize it without having to do much coding themselves. The downside of this is that if you cannot find what you are looking for, you will have to develop it yourself, and it is bound to be significantly less efficient than a preexisting package.

Python has a large user community and a plethora of tutorials and books, so learning it and mastering it is a straight-forward process. You can even find working scripts on the web from other users, so you often don't need to do much coding yourself. Moreover, it runs on pretty much every computer out there, even tiny PCs like Raspberry Pi and Arduino.

Apart from its overall low speed, Python has other issues, such as the fact that its loops are quite inefficient. Because of this, they are often a taboo of sorts. Also, the fact that there are two main versions of it (2.x and 3.x) makes it very confusing; there are good packages in one that are often not available to the other version. Even if the newest version of Python (right now, 3.6) is pretty robust for a high-level language, it lacks the packages that older versions of it have. Nevertheless, Python is widely popular and has established itself as a data science language, even if it is not the best one for this purpose.

R

There is some controversy over whether R is a programming language or not, due to the fact that it is not a multipurpose coding tool by any stretch. However, for all practical purposes, it is a programming language, albeit a weak one. R offers easy access to statistics and other data analysis tools, and requires little programming from the user. Just like Julia and Python, it is intuitive, and many people find it easy to learn, even if they do not have any programming experience. This is partly due to its exceptional IDE, RStudio, which is open-source. Although it was primarily designed for statistics and its target group has traditionally been academia, it has gained popularity in the data science community and has a large user base. The fact that it has some excellent plotting libraries may have contributed to this.

One major downside to R is that it is particularly slow. Another is the fact its for-loops are very slow, which are so much frowned upon that they are not even included in some R tutorials. Also, because of various reasons, including the fact that there are newcomers in the data science languages arena, R is on the wane lately. Still, it is a useful tool for small-scale data analytics, particularly if you just want to use it in a proof-of-concept project.

Scala

Just like Julia, Scala is a functional language with elements of object-oriented programming. As such, it is fairly future-proof, making it worthy as an investment of your time (particularly if you know Java). The reason for this is that Scala stems from Java and even runs on the JVM. Due to its clean code and its seamless integration with Apache Spark, it has a growing user community. Finally, it is fairly fast and easier to use than low-level languages, though not as intuitive as the other languages I mentioned in this section.

Unfortunately, Scala doesn't have many data science libraries since it has only been around for a few years. Also, it does not collaborate very well with other programming languages (apart from Java, of course). Finally, Scala is not easy to learn, although there are several books and tutorials out there demonstrating how it can be used for various applications. Generally, it is a useful language for data science, particularly if you are into the functional paradigm, if you have worked with Java before, or if you are fond of Spark.

Which Language is Best for You?

Unfortunately, there is no clear-cut answer to this question. It greatly depends on you, particularly your background. Here is a rule-of-thumb answer, as a guideline to what may be best for you in general.

If you are coming from academia, the language that would best suit you is R. Most likely you are already familiar with it, which is an obvious advantage. You will just need to get acquainted with its data science libraries, many of which are described in my first data science book, *Data Scientist* (http://bit.ly/2nHxeFA).

If you are fairly new to programming but are not satisfied with R, Python is a good language to use. Its large variety of tutorials and other educational material make it easy to learn, and its breadth of data science libraries will allow you to focus on high-level programming, at which this language is fairly good. A great book to get you started is *Python Data Science Essentials* by Luca Massaron and Alberto Boschetti (http://amzn.to/2mK4V8y).

If you are big on Spark, Java, and/or functional programming, then Scala is the language for you. You may want to use it in conjunction with some other language for prototyping, but if you are into functional programming, you probably know a high-level language already. Here are a couple of good tutorials for Scala that you may find useful: http://bit.ly/2nTpShx (Tutorials Point) and http://bit.ly/1WupbGx (YouTube).

Finally, if you want to do something fast and easy in data science, regardless of whether you have much programming experience or not, Julia is a great choice for you. You can learn it and its applicability in data science through the book *Julia for Data Science* by Technics Publications (http://bit.ly/2nGP8IA).

The Most Useful Packages for Julia and Python

Since Julia and Python dominate the data science world in terms of overall usefulness and ease of use, here is a list of libraries (packages) that are popular and/or useful for data science projects:

Python:
1. **NumPy** – You cannot do anything useful with Python without NumPy, as it provides the math essentials for any data-related project

2. **SciPy** – very useful package for math, with an emphasis on scientific computing
3. **Matplotlib** – 2-D plotting
4. **Pandas** – a package that allows for dataframe structures
5. **Statsmodels** – statistical models package, including one for regression
6. **Distance** – the go-to package for implementation of various distance metrics
7. **IPython** – Although not strictly data-related, it is essential for making Python easy to use, and it is capable of integrating with Jupyter notebooks
8. **scikit-learn** – collection of implementations of various machine learning and data mining algorithms
9. **Theano** – a package designed to facilitate computationally heavy processes using GPUs; useful for deep learning, among other resource-demanding applications
10. **NLTK** –Although its parts-of-speech (POS) tagging is sub-optimal, NLTK is an essential package for NLP, and it's easy to use with good documentation
11. **tsne** – the Python implementation of the T-SNE algorithm for reducing a dataset into 2-D and 3-D, for easier visualization
12. **Scrapy** – a useful web-scraping package
13. **Bokeh** – a great visualization package that allows for interactive plots
14. **NetworkX** – a very useful graph analytics package that is both versatile and scalable
15. **mxnet** – the Python API for the state-of-the-art deep learning framework, developed by Apache and used heavily on the Amazon cloud
16. **elm** – a package for developing Extreme Learning Machines systems, a not-so-well-known machine learning system
17. **tensorflow** – the Python API for the TensorFlow deep learning framework

Julia:
1. **StatsBase** – a collection of various statistics functions
2. **HypothesisTests** – a package containing several statistical methods for hypothesis testing
3. **Gadfly** – one of the best plotting packages, written entirely in Julia

4. **PyPlot** – a great plotting package, borrowed from Python's Matplotlib; ideal for heat maps
5. **Clustering** – a package specializing in clustering methods
6. **DecisionTree** – decision trees and random forests package
7. **Graphs** – a graph analytics package (the most complete one out there)
8. **LightGraphs** – a package with relatively fast graph algorithms
9. **DataFrames** – the equivalent of pandas for Julia
10. **Distances** – a very useful package for distance calculation, covering all major distance metrics
11. **GLM** – generalized linear model package for regression analysis
12. **TSNE** – a package implementing the T-SNE algorithm by the creators of the algorithm
13. **ELM** – the go-to package for Extreme Learning Machines, having a single hidden layer
14. **MultivariateStats** – a great place to obtain various useful statistics functions, including PCA
15. **MLBase** – an excellent resource for various support functions for ML applications
16. **MXNet** – the Julia API for mxnet, a great option for deep-learning applications
17. **TensorFlow** – the Julia API for the TensorFlow deep learning framework

Other Data Analytics Software

Apart from the aforementioned data analytics software, there are others that have a more specialized or niche role in data science. You do not need to know them in order to perform your projects, but you may hear about them and find companies that use them. These are mainly proprietary programs, so their user base is somewhat smaller than the communities of open-source software.

MATLAB

Back in the day, before all the current data science languages were a thing (apart from R, which has been around since the time of the dinosaurs), MATLAB was the way to go if you wanted to do any serious data analytics work. Even today, some people still use it, though it mainly appeals to the academic crowd. This is probably due to the fact that universities get a huge discount for its license, and because it is a fairly easy language to learn and work with. Over the years, many libraries have been developed for it, plus its GUI is one of the best out there. Its slick interface and ease of use could not justify the high price tag that it fetches, so its popularity has waned, especially after Julia entered the scene. Although hardly any data scientists use MATLAB any more, it is still the go-to framework for many researchers, and there is a lot of free code (.m files) available at the MathWorks site.

There are also a couple of open-source clones of MATLAB out there, for those unwilling to pay the expensive license fee. These are Octave and Scilab. Also, it is noteworthy that the SciPy package in Python borrows a lot of MATLAB's functionality, so it is a bit like MATLAB for Python users. Despite its issues, MATLAB is a great tool for data visualization, which is why it is sometimes preferred by researchers across different fields (especially if they receive a heavily discounted license through their academic institutions).

Analytica

This lesser-known software is one of the best programs out there for modeling processes in such a way that it enables even outsiders to understand what's happening. Analytica mimics the functionality of flowcharts, making them executable programs by adding code on the back-end. Although it seems old-fashioned these days due to the more traditional look-and-feel that it exhibits, it is still a useful tool, particularly for modeling and analyzing high-level data analytics processes.

Analytica is very intuitive and easy to use, and its visualization tools make it shine. However, it fetches a high price and doesn't collaborate with any other data analytics tools (apart from MS Excel), making it fairly unpopular among data scientists today. Still, it is much better than many other alternatives that require you to take a whole course in order to be able to do anything meaningful with them. There is a free version of it, able to handle small datasets, should you want to give it a try.

Mathematica

Poised more towards scientific analytics work, Mathematica is another niche software that lends itself to data analytics, perhaps more than other programs that specialize in the data science field. Its intuitive language that resembles Python and its excellent documentation make it the go-to option for anyone in the research industry who wants to create a functional model of the phenomenon being studied. It would be unfair to compare it with MATLAB though, as some people do, since Mathematica is able to do abstract math too. Additionally, its plotting capabilities make one wonder if this is actually a visualization tool. Even more, all of its functionality is embedded in its kernel, meaning that you don't have to worry about finding, installing, and loading the right package for your task.

If it weren't for its name, which implies a mathematics-oriented application, Mathematica would probably have gotten more traction in the data science community. Its high price doesn't help its case either. Nevertheless, if you find yourself in a company that has invested in a license for it, then it would be worth learning it in depth through its numerous educational materials that are made available on the Wolfram site, as well as on Amazon. Also, its interface is so well-designed that you do not need any programming background to carry out meaningful tasks, though if you do know a programming language already, it would be much easier to learn.

Visualization Software

One thing I hope became abundantly clear from Chapter 2 is that visualization is big on the data science pipeline. What good are all the insights you create if they are not delivered properly with the help of visuals that are both insightful and possibly even impressive? This is particularly important if data science is new in the organization you work for and needs to assert itself there, or if you are new to the field. Even if you cannot hide lack of usefulness behind a pretty plot, you may need to get your graphics as glamorous as possible if you are to drive home the point you are trying to make in the final stage of the pipeline. Fortunately, there are several tools out there that specialize in just that. Here are some of the more widely known ones.

Plot.ly

The Canadian company that came up with this visualization tool must have really known what they were doing, because their product is by far the best visualization tool out there. Its key benefit is that it allows you to work your plots in different platforms, while also being easy to use, and the quality of these plots is quite good. If you plan to share your graphics with other people who prefer to use a different programming language but who may want to add or change them, Plot.ly is the way to go. Even the free edition is good enough to make a difference, although if you want to create something more professional, like a dashboard, you will need to pay a certain amount per month to take advantage of the full set of features this tool has.

D3.js

This is a JavaScript library that allows for professional-looking graphics for your data. Employing HTML, CSS, and other web technologies, it is a very accessible, open-source tool. You can download it as a .zip file and make use of its scripts in the web page documents you create with it to showcase your plots. Its key features are that it is very fast, supports a variety of datasets, and allows for animations as well as interactive plots. On its website (www.d3js.org), you can find tutorials as well as examples.

WolframAlpha

The same company that created Mathematica has also developed a search engine specializing in knowledge (that is related to science and engineering). One of the features of this online product is data visualization. Although it is not ideal for this kind of application, it is good enough for some data exploration tasks, especially considering that it is free and that it is primarily designed for knowledge retrieval rather than anything data science related. It will be interesting to see how it evolves, considering that Wolfram Inc. has been looking at expanding its domain to include data science applications. The Wolfram language lends itself to it, as it is now armed with a series of machine learning algorithms alongside the ones for interactive plots.

Tableau

Tableau is used to create professional-looking plots for BI professionals and data scientists alike. Although there are also free versions of it available, if you want to do anything meaningful with it, you need to have one of the paid versions. Whatever the case, it is popular, so you will likely encounter several companies that require it as a skill (even though there are several better and cheaper alternatives out there, including some open-source ones).

Data Governance Software

Data governance involves storing, managing, and processing data in a distributed environment, something essential when it comes to big data. There are several options for this, so a lot of the low-level work has been abstracted through user-friendly interfaces, making the whole process much easier. The key data governance software out there include Spark, Hadoop, and Storm. There are also other ones available that may be useful, even if they are not as popular.

Spark

There is little doubt nowadays that Spark is the best way to go when it comes to data governance, even if it is still a fairly new framework. Its increased popularity over the past years is remarkable, and its integration with Python and R is a big plus. Still, if you want to do serious work with it, you may want to pick up Scala, since that's the language it is most compatible with (Spark is also written in that language). The key advantages of Spark are generality (it can be used for different data science applications, not just data analytics tasks), versatility (it can be run on different environments, such as Hadoop clusters, Amazon's S3 infrastructure, and more), speed (it is significantly faster than its alternatives), ease of use (it makes use of a high-level programming paradigm and can be used from within your programming language by importing the corresponding package), and has a vibrant community of users. Despite its simplicity, Spark covers various verticals of data governance, the most important of which are:

- Data querying through a SQL-like language and a robust data frames system (Spark SQL)
- Machine learning analytics (MLlib)
- Graph analytics (GraphX)
- Stream analysis (Spark Streaming)

Hadoop

Hadoop is the most established big data platform. Although lately it has been on the wane, many companies still use it, and there are plenty of data scientists who swear by it. Geared toward the traditional cluster-based approach to big data governance, Hadoop appeals more to very large organizations with lots of computers linked to each other. Its various components are low-level, yet they are manageable by several programming languages through APIs. The main aspects of the Hadoop ecosystem are:

- **MapReduce** – the main algorithm for splitting a task into smaller sub-tasks, spreading them across the various nodes of the computer cluster, and then fusing the results
- **JobTracker** – the coordinator program of the various parallel processes across the cluster
- **HDFS** (Hadoop Distributed File System) – the file system for managing files stored in a cluster
- **HBase** – Hadoop's NoSQL database system
- **Hive** – a query platform for Hadoop databases
- **Mahout** – a machine learning platform
- **Pig** – Hadoop's scripting language
- **Sqoop** – Hadoop's data integration component
- **Oozie** – a workflow and scheduling system for Hadoop jobs
- **ZooKeeper** – Hadoop coordination component
- **Ambari** – a management and monitoring tool for the Hadoop ecosystem

Storm

Storm comes from the same company that developed Spark (Apache) and focuses on handling data that moves at high speeds (each node of a cluster running Storm can process over a million tuples per second). Its simplicity, ease of use, and versatility in terms of programming languages make it an appealing option for many people. The fact that it is scalable, fault-tolerant, and quite user-friendly in terms of setting up and using makes it a great tool to be familiar with, even if you will not use it in every data science project you undertake.

Version Control Systems (VCS)

Version control is an important matter in all situations where more than one person works on the same code base for a project. Although it may sometimes be unnecessary when working on a project by yourself, it is often the case that you need to revert to previous versions of your programs, so a version control system can be useful in this case. A VCS can be either centralized (i.e. all of the repository is in a centralized location), or decentralized (i.e. the data is spread out across various computers). Lately, the focus is on the latter category, as it has several advantages over the centralized VCS.

Chances are that the organization you work for will have a VCS in place and will already be committed to it, as such frameworks are very popular among software developers. Since you may often be working with them, you will be expected to know at least one of the most well-known such systems, namely Git, Github, and CVS. Let's take a closer look at each one.

Git

Git is one of the more established VCS out there, and it was developed by Linus Torvalds, who is also the creator of the Linux kernel, used widely across all kinds of devices (including most smart phones) as the core component of their operating system. Although this may have contributed to Git's popularity, the fact is that it is so easy to learn, has so much educational material out there (including lots of videos), and is so widespread in the industry that it is the go-to VCS for the majority of coding applications, including data science. Also, although there are GUIs out there for it, most of the users prefer to use the command line interface for it, alongside its cloud counterpart, Github. Although these two are often used in conjunction, Git is compatible with other cloud storage platforms too, such as Dropbox.

Just like most VCS, Git is open-source and has a respectable-sized community around it and is cross-platform. If you are still not convinced about its usefulness, it is also being used by a variety of companies, like Microsoft,

Facebook, Twitter, Android/Google, and Netflix. You can learn more about it at its official website: https://git-scm.com.

Github

Github is probably the most commonly used VCS, both among developers and data scientists. Although it is not in any way superior to Git, it is still a good VCS, especially if you are not fond of the command line interface. Github's key selling points (it is not free if you want to take advantage of its most important features, such as private repositories) are that it allows for easy coding reviews, provides end-to-end encryption, and makes changes/branches in the code more manageable. This means that through the comments, you are encouraged to include all your code revisions and the difference-tracking system the system provides, and you can easily revert to previous versions of your programs as well as examine the variations of your current script from an earlier one. Github also allows for easy sharing of your code, as most programmers have an account there (oftentimes even companies including Julia Computing publish their material there). Bottom line, even if you decide to use something else as a VCS, it is a good idea to become intimately acquainted with Github; chances are, you will visit it at one point.

CVS

This is one of the most well-known centralized VCS. Just like Git, it is free and fairly easy to use. Its key advantages over other (centralized) VCS are the following:

- It allows the running for logging scripts
- It enables its users to have local versions of their files (vendor branches), something useful for large teams
- Several people can work on the same file simultaneously
- Entire collections of files can be manipulated with a single command, allowing for a modular approach to version control

- It works on most Unix-like operating systems, as well as on different versions of Windows

---

Summary

Databases are important in data science, and all of the ones you'll encounter fit in one of three categories:

- SQL
- NoSQL
- Graph-based

Programming languages in data science are a key tool, as you will probably rely on them the most in your projects. The most common are:

- Julia
- Python
- R
- Scala

Beyond the conventional open-source programming platforms, there are also other data analytics tools that are used in some places:

- MATLAB
- Analytica
- Mathematica

There are several visualization options out there beyond the built-in ones in the programming language(s) you use. The most noteworthy of them are:

- Plot.ly
- D3.js
- Tableau

Data governance is very important in data science, especially when dealing with big data. The tools that stand out in this category are:

- Spark
- Hadoop
- Storm

Version Control System (VCS) software is also important when working in a team that handles the same scripts and project files in general. The VCS most commonly used are:

- Git
- Github
- CVS

PART 2

Setting the Stage for Data Analytics

CHAPTER 5

Data Science Questions and Hypotheses

Although everyone talks about the data science pipeline, the data scientist's toolbox, and all the great things that data science can do for you, few data science professionals bother talking about one of the most essential means of tackling data science problems: questions. This is probably because it is less high-tech than other parts of the craft, while it is perceived as a less data science savvy task. This is however, yet another misconception about the field.

Questions in data science may stem from a project manager to some extent, but most of them come from you. The only way to find answers to your questions is through the data you have, so the questions need to be constructed and processed in such a way that they are answerable and able to yield useful information that can help guide your project. This whole process involves the creation of hypotheses, the formal scientific means for turning these questions into something that can be tackled in an objective manner.

In this chapter, we will look at what kinds of questions we can ask and which hypotheses correspond to them. Furthermore, in later chapters, we'll delve deeper into this matter to see how we can turn these questions into a source of useful information through experiments and the analysis of the results.

Importance of Asking (the Right) Questions

Although the people who drive the data science projects are usually the ones who ask the key questions that need to be answered through these projects, you need to ask your own questions for two reasons:

1. The questions your superiors ask tend to be more general and very hard to answer directly, leading to potential miscommunications or inadequate understanding of the underlying problem being investigated
2. As you work with the various data streams at your disposal, you gain a better understanding of problems and can ask more informative (specialized) questions that can get into the heart of the data at hand

Now you may ask "What's the point of asking questions in data science if the use of AI can solve so many problems for us?" Many people who are infatuated with AI tend to think that, and as a result, consider questions a secondary part of data science, if not something completely irrelevant. Although the full automation of certain processes through AI may be a great idea for a sci-fi film, it has little to do with the reality and truth. Artificial Intelligence can be a great aid in data science work, but it is not at a stage where it can do all the work for us. That's why, regardless of how sophisticated the AI systems are, they cannot ask questions that are meaningful or useful, nor can they communicate them to anyone in a comprehensive and intuitive way.

Sometimes it helps to think of such things with metaphors so that we obtain a more concrete understanding of the corresponding concepts. Think of AI as a good vehicle that can take you from A to B in a reliable and efficient manner. Yet, even if it is a state-of-the-art car (e.g. a self-driving one), it still needs to know where B is. Finding this is a matter of asking the right questions, something that AI is unable to do in its current state.

As insights come in all shapes and forms, it is important to remember that some of them can only be accessed by going deeper into the data. These insights also tend to be more targeted and valuable, so it's definitely worth the extra effort. After all, it's easy to find the low-hanging fruit of a given problem! To obtain these more challenging insights, you need to perform in-depth analysis that go beyond data exploration. An essential part of this endeavor is formulating questions about the different aspects of the data at hand. Failing to do that is equivalent to providing conventional data analytics (e.g. business intelligence, or econometrics), which although fine in and of itself, is not data science, and passing it as data science would undermine your role and reputation.

Naturally, all these questions need to be grounded in a way that is both formal and unambiguous. In other words, there needs to be some scientific rigor in them and a sense of objectivity as to how they can be tackled. That's where hypotheses enter the scene, namely the scientific way of asking questions and expanding one's knowledge of the problem studied. These are the means that allow for finding something useful, in a practical way, with the questions you come up with, while pondering on the data.

Finally, asking questions and formulating hypotheses underline the human aspect of data science in a very hands-on way. Data may look like ones and zeros when handled by the computer, but it is more than that. Otherwise, everything could be fully automated by a machine (which it can't, at least not yet). It is this subtleness in the data and the information it contains that make asking questions even more important and useful in every data science project.

Formulating a Hypothesis

Once you have your question down, you are ready to turn it into something your data is compatible with, namely a hypothesis. A hypothesis is something you can test in a methodical and objective manner. In fact, most scientific research is done through the use of different kinds of hypotheses that are then tested against measurements (experimental data) and in some cases theories (refined information and knowledge). In data science, we usually focus on the experimental evidence.

Formulating a hypothesis is fairly simple as long as the question is quantifiable. You must make a statement that summarizes the question in a very conservative way (basically something like the negation of the statement you use as a question).

The statement that takes the form of the hypothesis is always a yes-or-no question, and it's referred to as the *Null Hypothesis* (usually denoted as *H0*). This is what you opt to disprove later on by gathering enough evidence against it.

Apart from the Null Hypothesis, you also need to formulate another hypothesis, which is what would be a potential answer to the question at hand. This is called the *Alternative Hypothesis* (symbolized as *Ha*), and although you can never prove it 100%, if you gather enough evidence to disprove the Null Hypothesis, the chances of the Alternative Hypothesis being valid are better. It is often the case that there are many possibilities beyond that of the Null Hypothesis, so this whole process needs to be repeated several times in order to obtain an answer with a reasonable level of confidence. We'll examine this dynamic in more detail in the following chapter. For now, let's look at the most common questions you can ask and how you can formulate hypotheses based on them.

Questions Related to Most Common Use Cases

Naturally, not all questions are suitable for data science projects. Also, certain questions lend themselves more to the discovery of insights, as they are more easily quantifiable and closer to the essence of the data at hand, as opposed to other questions that aim to mainly facilitate our understanding of the problem.

In general, the more specific a question is and the closer it is related to the available data, the more valuable it tends to be. Specifically, we can ask questions related to the relationship between two features, the difference between two subsets of a variable, how well two variables in a feature set collaborate with each other for predicting another variable, whether a variable ought to be removed from the set, how similar two variables are to each other, whether variable X causes the phenomenon mirrored in variable Y to occur, and more. Let's now look at each one of these types of question in more detail.

Is Feature X Related to Feature Y?

This is one of the simplest questions to ask and can yield very useful information about your feature set and the problem in general. Naturally, you can ask the same question with other variables in the dataset, such as the target ones. However, since usually you cannot do much about the target variables, more often than not you would ask questions like this by focusing on features. This way, if you find that feature X is very closely related to feature Y, you may decide to remove X or Y from your dataset, since it doesn't add a great deal of information. You can think of it as having two people in a meeting that always agree. However, before taking any action based on the answer you obtain about the relationship between these two features, it is best to examine other features as well, especially if the features themselves are fairly rich in terms of the information they contain.

The hypothesis you can formulate based on this kind of question is also fairly simple. You can hypothesize that the values of these features are of the same population (i.e. H0: the similarity between the values of X and Y is zero).

If the features are continuous, it is important to normalize them first, as well as remove any outliers they may have (especially if you are using a basic metric to measure their relationship). Otherwise, depending on how different the scale is or how different the values of the outliers are in relation to the other values, you may find the two features different when they are not. Also, the similarity is usually measured by a specific metric designed for this task. The alternative to this hypothesis would be that the two features are not of the same population (i.e. Ha: there is a measurable similarity between the values of X and Y).

If this whole process is new to you, it helps to write your hypotheses down so that you can refer to them easily afterwards. However, as you get more used to them, you can just make a mental note about the hypotheses you formulate as you ask your questions.

An example of this type of question is as follows: we have two features in a dataset, a person's age (X1) and that person's work experience (X2). Although they correspond to two different things, they may be quite related. The question therefore would be, "Is there a relationship between a person's age and their work experience?" Here are the hypotheses we can formulate to answer this question accurately:

```
H0: there is no measurable relationship between X1 and X2

Ha: X1 is related to X2
```

Although the answer may be intuitive to us, we cannot be sure unless we test these hypotheses, since the data at hand may have a different story to tell about how these two variables relate to each other.

Is Subset X Significantly Different to Subset Y?

This is a very useful question to ask when you are examining the values of a variable in more depth. In fact, you can't do any serious data analysis without asking and answering this question. The subsets X and Y are usually derived from the same variable, but they can come from any variable of your dataset, as long as both of them are of the same type (e.g. both are integers).

However, usually X and Y are parts of a continuous variable. As such, they are both of the same scale, so no normalization is required. Also it is usually the case that any outliers that may exist in that variable have been either removed or changed to adapt to the variable's distribution. So, X and Y are in essence two sets of float numbers that may or may not be different enough as quantities to imply that they are really parts of two entirely different populations. Whether they are or not will depend on how different these values are. In other words, say we have the following hypothesis that we want to check:

```
H0: the difference between X and Y is insubstantial (more
or less zero)
```

The alternative hypothesis in this case would be:

```
Ha: the difference between X and Y is substantial (greater
than zero in absolute value)
```

Note that it doesn't matter if X is greater than Y or if Y is greater than X. All we want to find out is if one of them is substantially larger than the other, since regardless of which one is larger, the two subsets will be different enough. This "enough" part is something measurable, usually through a statistic, and if this statistic exceeds a certain threshold, it is referred to as "significant" in scientific terms.

If X and Y stem from a discrete variable, it requires a different approach to answer this question, but the hypothesis formulated is the same. We'll look into the underlying differences between these two cases in the next chapter.

Do Features X and Y Collaborate Well with Each Other for Predicting Variable Z?

This is a very useful question to ask. Many people don't realize they could ask it, while others have no idea how they could answer it properly. Whatever the case, it's something worth keeping in mind, especially if you are dealing with a predictive analytics problem with lots of features. It doesn't matter if it's a classification, a regression, or even a time-series, when you have several features, chances are that some of them don't help much in the prediction, even if they are good predictors on their own.

Of course, how well two features collaborate depend on the problem they are applied on. So, it is important to first decide on the problem and on the metric you'll rely on primarily for the performance of your model. For classification, you'll probably go for F1 and Area Under Curve (AUC, relating to the ROC curve). In this sense, the collaboration question can be viewed from the perspective of the evaluation metric's value. Therefore, the question can take the form of the following hypothesis (which like before, we need to see if we can disprove):

```
H0: the addition of feature Y does not affect the value of
evaluation metric M when using just X in the predictive
model
```

The alternative hypothesis would be:

```
Ha: adding Y as a feature in a model consisting only of X
will cause considerable improvement to performance of the
model, as measured by evaluation metric M.
```

Also, the following set of hypotheses would also be worth using, to formalize the same question:

```
H0: the removal of feature Y does not affect the value of
evaluation metric M when using both X and Y in the
predictive model

Ha: removing Y from a model consisting of X and Y will
cause considerable degradation in its performance, as
measured by evaluation metric M
```

Note that in both of these approaches to creating a hypothesis, we took into account the direction of the change in the performance metric's value. This is because the underlining assumption of features X and Y collaborating is that having them work in tandem is better than either one of them working on its own, as measured by our evaluation metric M.

Should We Remove X from the Feature Set?

After pondering the potential positive effect of a feature on a model, the question that comes to mind naturally is the reciprocal of that: would removing a feature, say X, from the feature set be good for the model (i.e. improve its performance)? Or in other words, should we remove X from the feature set for this particular problem? If you have understood the dynamics of feature collaboration underlined in the previous section, this question and its hypothesis should be fairly obvious. Yet, most people don't pay enough attention to it, opting for more automated ways to reduce the number of features, oftentimes without realizing what is happening in the process.

If you would rather not take shortcuts and you would prefer to have a more intimate understanding of the dynamics in play, you may want to explore this question more. This will not only help you explain why you let go of feature X, but also gain some insight on the dynamics of features in a predictive analytics model in general. So, when should you take X out of the feature set? Well, there are two distinct possibilities:

1. X degrades the performance of the model (as measured by evaluation metric M)

2. The model's performance remains the same whether X is present or not (based on the same metric)

One way of encapsulating this in a hypothesis setting is the following:

```
H0: having X in the model makes its performance, based on
evaluation metric M, notably higher than omitting it from
the model

Ha: removing X from the model either improves or maintains
the same performance, as measured by metric M
```

Like in the previous question type, it is important to remember that the usefulness of a feature greatly depends on the problem at hand. If you find that removing feature X is the wisest choice, it's best to still keep it around (i.e. don't delete it altogether), since it may be valuable as a feature in another problem, or perhaps with some mathematical tinkering.

How Similar are Variables X and Y?

Another question worth asking is related to the first one we covered in the chapter, namely the measure of the similarity of two variables X and Y. While answering whether the variables are related may be easy, we may be interested in finding out exactly how much they are related. This is not based on some arbitrary mathematical sense of curiosity. It has a lot of hands-on applications in different data science scenarios, such as predictive analytics. For example, in a regression problem, finding out *how similar* a feature X is to the target variable Y is a good sign that it ought to be included in the model. Also, in any problem that involves continuous variables as features, finding that two such variables are very similar to each other may lead us to omit one of them, even without having to go through the process of the previous section, thus saving time.

In order to answer this question, we tend to rely on similarity metrics, so it's usually not the case that we formulate hypotheses for this sort of question. Besides, most statistical similarity metrics come with a set of statistics that help clarify the significance of the result. However, even though this is a possibility, the way statistics has modeled the whole similarity matter is both arbitrary and weak, at least for real-world situations, so we'll refrain from examining this approach. Besides, twisting the data into a preconceived idea of how it should be (i.e. a statistics distribution) may be convenient, but data science opts to deal with the data as-is rather than how we'd like it to be. Therefore, it is best to measure similarity with various metrics (particularly ones that don't make any assumptions about the distributions of the variables involved) rather than rely on some statistical method only.

Similarity metrics are a kind of heuristics designed to depict how closely related two features are on a scale of 0 to 1. You can think of them as the opposite of distances. We'll look at all of these along with other interesting metrics in detail in the heuristics chapter toward the last part of this book.

Does Variable X Cause Variable Y?

Whether a phenomenon expressed through variable X is the root-cause of a phenomenon denoted by variable Y is a tough problem to solve, and it is definitely beyond the scope of this book, yet a question related to this is quite valid and worth asking (this kind of problem is usually referred to as root-cause analysis). Nevertheless, unless you have some control over the whole data acquisition pipeline linked to the data science one, you may find it an unsurmountable task. The reason is that in order to prove or disprove causality, you need to carry out a series of experiments designed for this particular purpose, collect the data from them, and then do your analytics work. This is why more often than not, when opting to investigate this kind of question, we go for a simpler set-up known as A-B testing. This is not as robust, and it merely provides evidence of a contribution of the phenomenon of variable X in that of variable Y, which is quite different than saying that X is the root-cause of Y. Nevertheless, it is still a valuable method as it provides us with useful insights about the relationship between the two variables in a way that correlation metrics cannot.

A-B testing is the investigation of what happens when a control variable has a certain value in one case and a different value in another. The difference in the target variable Y between these two cases can show whether X influences Y in some measurable way. This is a much different question than the original one of this section. Still, it is worth looking into it, as it is common in practice.

The hypothesis that corresponds to this question is fairly simple. One way of formulating the null hypothesis is as follows:

```
H0: X does not influence Y in any substantial way
```

The alternative hypothesis in this case would be something like:

```
Ha: X contributes to Y in a substantial way
```

So, finding out if X is the root-cause of Y constitutes first checking to see if it influences Y, and then eliminating all other potential causes of Y one by one. To illustrate how complex this kind of analysis can be, consider that determining that smoking cigarettes is beyond a doubt a root cause of cancer (something that seems obvious to us now) took several years of research. Note that in the majority of cases of this kind of analysis, at least one of the variables (X, Y) is discrete.

Other Question Types

Apart from these question categories, there are several others that are more niche and therefore beyond the scope of this chapter (e.g. questions relevant to graph analysis, data mining, and other methodologies discussed previously). Nevertheless, you should explore other possibilities of questions and hypotheses so that at the very least, you develop a habit of doing that in your data science projects. This is bound to help you cultivate a more inquisitive approach to data analysis, something that is in and of itself an important aspect of the data science mindset.

Questions Not to Ask

Questions that are very generic or too open-ended should not be asked about the data. For example, questions like "What's the best methodology to use?" or "What's the best feature in the feature set?" or "Should I use more data for the model?" are bound to merely waste your time if you try to answer them using the data as is. The reason is that these questions are quite generic or their answers tend to be void of valuable information. For example, even if you find out that the best feature in the feature set is feature X, what good will that do? Besides, a feature's value often depends on the model you use, as well as how it collaborates with other features.

You may still want to answer these questions, but you will need to consult external sources of information (e.g. the client), or make them more specific. For example, the second question can be transformed into these questions, which make more sense: "What's the best feature in the feature set for predicting target variable X, if all other features are ignored?" or "What's the feature that adds the most value in the prediction of target variable X, given the existing model?"

Also, questions that have a sense of bias in them are best to be avoided, as they may distort your understanding of the problem. For example, "How much better is model A from model B in this problem?" makes the assumption that model A is indeed better than model B, so it may not allow you to be open to the possibility that it's not.

Also, very complex questions with many conditions in them are not too helpful either. Although they are usually quite specific, they may be complicated when it comes to testing them. So, unless you are adept in logic, you are better off tackling simpler questions that are easier to work with and answer.

Summary

Asking questions is essential since the questions given by the project managers are usually not enough or too general to guide you through the data science process of a given problem most effectively.

Formulating a hypothesis is an essential part of answering the questions you come up with, as it allows for a rigorous testing that can provide a more robust answer that is as unbiased as possible.

Hypotheses are generally yes or no questions that are subject to statistical testing so that they can be answered in a clear-cut way, and the result is accompanied by a confidence measure.

There are various kinds of questions you can ask. Some of the most common ones are:

- Is feature X related to feature Y?
- Is subset X significantly different from subset Y?
- Do features X and Y collaborate well with each other for predicting variable Z?
- Should we remove X from the feature set?
- How similar are variables X and Y?
- Does variable X cause variable Y?

CHAPTER 6

Data Science Experiments and Evaluation of Their Results

So, you've come up with a promising question for your data, and you have formulated a hypothesis around it (actually you'd probably have come up with a couple of them). Now what? Well, now it's time to test it and see if the results are good enough to make the alternative hypothesis you have proposed (Ha) a viable answer. This fairly straight-forward process is something we will explore in detail in this chapter, before we delve deeper into it in the chapter that ensues.

The Importance of Experiments

Experiments are essential in data science, and not just for testing a hypothesis. In essence, they are the means of the application of the scientific method, an empirical approach to obtaining refined knowledge objectively in order to acquire and process information. Also, it is the make-or-break way of validating a theory and the most concrete differentiator of science and philosophy as well as data science and the speculation of "experts" in a given domain. Experiments may be challenging, and their results may not always comply with our expectations or agree with our intuition. Still, they are always insightful and gradually advance our understanding of things, especially in complex scenarios or cases where we don't have sufficient domain knowledge.

In more practical terms, experiments are what make a concept we have grasped or constructed either a fact or a fleeting error in judgment. This not only provides us with confidence in our perception, but also allows for a more rigorous and somewhat objective approach to data analytics. Many people have lost faith in the results of statistics and for good reason. They tend to draw conclusions that are so dependent on assumptions that they fail to have value in the real world.

The pseudo-scientists that often make use of this tool do so only to propagate their misconceptions rather than do proper scientific work. In spite of all that, there are parts of statistics that are useful in data science, and one of them is the testing of hypotheses. Experiments are complementary to that, and since they are closely linked to these statistical tests, we'll group them together for the purpose of this chapter.

How to Construct an Experiment

First of all, let's clarify what we mean by experiments, since sci-fi culture may have tainted your perception of them. Experiments in data science are usually a form of a series of simulations you perform on a computer, typically in an environment like Jupyter (http://bit.ly/2oriE8B). Optionally, you can conduct all of your experiments from the command line. The environment you use is not so important, though if you are comfortable with a notebook setting, this would be best, as that kind of environment allows for the inclusion of descriptive text and graphics along with several other options, such as exporting the whole thing as a PDF or an HTML file.

Constructing an experiment entails the following things. If it's a fairly straight-forward question that you plan to answer and everything is formulated as a clear-cut hypothesis, the experiment will take the form of a statistical test or a series of such tests (in the case that you have several alternative hypotheses).

The statistical tests that are more commonly used are the t-test and the chi-square test. The former works on continuous variables, while the latter is suitable for discrete ones. Oftentimes, it is the case that you employ several tests to gain a deeper understanding of the hypotheses you want to check, particularly if the probability value (p-value) of the test is close to the threshold.

I recommend that you avoid using statistical tests like the z-test, unless you are certain that the underlining assumptions hold true (e.g. the distribution of each variable is Gaussian). If it is a more complex situation you are dealing with, you may need to do several simulations and then do a statistical test on the outputs of these simulations. We'll look into this case in more detail in the section that follows.

Something that may seem obvious is that every scientific experiment has to be reproducible. This doesn't mean that another experiment based on the same data is going to output the exact same results, but the new results should be close to the original ones. In other words, the conclusion should be the same no matter who performs the experiment, even if they use a different sample of the available data. If the experiment is not reproducible, you need to re-examine your process and question the validity of your conclusions. We are going to look more into this matter in the next chapter.

Another thing worth noting when it comes to constructing an experiment is that just like everything else you do throughout the data science pipeline, your experiments need to be accompanied by documentation. You don't need to write a great deal of text or anything particularly refined, as this documentation is bound to remain unseen by the stakeholders of the project, but if someone reads it, they will want to get the gist of things quickly.

Therefore, the documentation of your experiment is better off being succinct and focusing on the essential aspects of the tasks involved, much like the comments in the code of your scripts. In addition, even if you don't share the documentation with anyone, it is still useful since you may need to go back to square one at some point and re-examine what you have done. Moreover, this documentation can be useful when writing up your report for the project, as well as any supplementary material for it, such as slideshow presentations.

Experiments for Assessing the Performance of a Predictive Analytics System

When it comes to assessing the performance of a predictive analytics system, we must take a specific approach to setting up the experiments needed to check if the models we create are good enough to put into production. Although this makes use of statistical testing, it goes beyond that, as these experiments must take into account the data used in these models as well as a set of metrics.

One way to accomplish this is through the use of sampling methods. The most popular such method is K-fold cross validation, which is a robust way of splitting the dataset in training and testing K times, minimizing the bias of the samples generated. When it comes to classification problems, the sampling that takes place takes into account the class distribution, something particularly useful if there is an imbalance there. This sort of sampling is referred to as *stratified sampling*, and it is more robust than conventional random sampling (although stratified sampling has a random element to it too, just like most sampling methods).

When you are trying out a model and want to examine if it's robust enough, you'll need to do a series of trainings and testings of that model using different subsets of the dataset and calculating a performance metric after each run. Then you can aggregate all the values of this metric and compare them to a baseline or a desired threshold value, using some statistical test. It is strongly recommended that you gather at least 30 such values before trying out a statistical evaluation of them, since the reliability of the results of the experiment depends on the amount of data points you have. Oftentimes, this experimental setup is in conjunction with the K-fold cross validation method mentioned previously, for an even more robust result. Experiments of this kind are so vigorous that their results tend to be trustworthy enough to render a scientific publication (particularly if the model you use is something new or a novel variant of an existing predictive analytics system).

Since simulations like these often take some time to run, particularly if you are running them on a large dataset, you may want to include more than one performance metrics. Popular metrics to measure performance are F1 for classification and MSE for regression or time-series analysis. In addition, if you have several models you wish to test, you may want to include all of them in the same experiment so you can run each of them on the same data as the others. This subtle point that is often neglected can add another layer of robustness to your experiments, as no one can say that the model you selected as having the best performance simply lucked out. If you have enough runs, the probability of one model outperforming the others due primarily to chance diminishes greatly.

A Matter of Confidence

Confidence is an important matter, not just as a psychological attribute, but also in the way the questions to the data are answered through this experiment-oriented process. The difference is that in this latter case, we can have a reliable measure of confidence, which has a very important role in the hypothesis testing process, namely quantifying the answer. What's more, you don't need to be a particularly confident person to exercise confidence in your data science work when it comes to this kind of task. You just need to do your due diligence when tackling this challenge and be methodical in your approach to the tests.

Confidence is usually expressed in a heuristic metric that takes the form of a confidence score, having values ranging between 0 and 1. This corresponds to the probability of the system's prediction being correct (or within an acceptable range of error). When it comes to statistical methods, this confidence score is the inverse of the p-value of the statistical metric involved. Yet, no matter how well-defined all these confidence metrics are, their scope is limited and dependent on the dataset involved. This is one of the reasons why it is important to make use of a diverse and balanced dataset when trying to answer questions about the variables involved.

It is often the case that we need to pinpoint a given metric, such as the average value of a variable or its standard deviation. This variable may be a mission-critical or key-performance index. In cases like this, we tend to opt for a confidence interval, something that ensures a given confidence level for a range of values for the metric we are examining. More often than not, this interval's level of confidence is set to 95%, yet it can take any value, usually near that point. Whatever the case, its value directly depends on the p-value threshold we have chosen a-priori (e.g. in this case, 0.05). Note that although statistics are often used for determining this interval, it doesn't have to be this way. Nowadays, more robust, assumption-free methods, such as Monte-Carlo simulations, are employed for deriving the exact borders of a confidence interval for any distribution of data.

Regardless of what methods you make use of for answering a data science question, it is important to keep in mind that you can never be 100% certain about your answer. The confidence score is bound to be less than 1, even if you use a large number of iterations in your experiments or a large number of data points in general. For all practical purposes, however, a high enough confidence score is usually good enough for the project. After all, data science is more akin to engineering than pure mathematics, since just like all other applied sciences, data science focuses on being realistic and practical.

Embracing this ambiguity in the conclusions is a necessary step and a differentiator of the data science mindset from the other, more precision-focused disciplines of science. In addition, this ambiguity is abundant in big data, which is one of the factors that make data science a priceless tool for dealing with this kind of data. However, doing more in-depth analysis through further testing can help tackle a large part of this ambiguity and shed some light on the complex problems of big data by making it a bit more ordered and concrete.

Finally, it is essential to keep in mind when answering a question that even if you do everything right, you may still be wrong in your conclusions. This counter-intuitive situation could be because the data used was of low veracity, or it wasn't cleaned well enough, or maybe parts of the dataset were stale. All these possibilities go on to demonstrate that data science is not an exact science, especially if the acquisition of the data at hand is beyond the control of the data scientist, as is often the case.

This whole discipline has little room for arrogance; do not rely more on fancy techniques than a solid understanding of the field. It is good to remember this, particularly when communicating your conclusions. You should not expect any groundbreaking discoveries unless you have access to large volumes of diverse, reliable, and information-rich data, along with sufficient computing resources to process it properly.

Evaluating the Results of an Experiment

The results of the experiment can be obtained in an automated way, especially if the experiment is fairly simple. However, evaluating these results and understanding how to best act on them is something that requires attention. That's because evaluation and interpretation of the results are closely intertwined. If done properly, there is little room for subjectivity. Let's look into this in more detail by examining the two main types of experiments we covered in this chapter, statistical tests and performance of predictive analytics models, and how we can evaluate the results in each case.

If it is a statistical test that you wish to interpret the results of, you just need to examine the various statistics that came along with it. The one that stands out the most, since it is the one yielding the most relevant information, is the p-value, which we talked about previously. This is a float number which takes values between 0 and 1 (inclusive) and denotes the probability of the result being caused by chance alone (i.e. the aggregation of various factors that were not accounted for, which contributed to it, even if you were not aware of their role or even their existence). The reason this is so important is that even in a controlled experiment, it is possible that the corresponding result has been strongly influenced by all the other variables that were not taken into account. If the end-result is caused by them, then the p-value is high, and that's bad news for our test. Otherwise, it should take a fairly small value (the smaller the better for the experiment). In general, we use 0.05 (5%) as the cut-off point, below which we consider the result statistically significant. If you find this threshold a bit too high, you can make use of other popular values for it, such as 0.01, 0.001, or even lower ones.

If you are dealing with the evaluation of the performance of a classifier, a regressor, or some other predictive analytics system, you just need to gather all the data from the evaluation metric(s) you plan to use for all the systems you wish to test and put that data into a matrix. Following this, you can run a series of tests (usually a t-test would work very well for this sort of data) to find out which model's performance, according to the given performance metrics, is both higher than the others and with a statistical significance. The data you will be using will correspond to columns in the aforementioned matrix. Make sure you calculate the standard deviation or the variance of each column in advance though, since in certain tests, having equal variances is a parameter in the test itself.

As we saw in the previous chapter, there are cases where a similarity metric makes more sense for answering a question. These kinds of metrics usually take values between 0 and 1, or between -1 and 1. In general, the higher the absolute value of the metric, the stronger the signal in the relationship examined. In most cases, this translates into a more affirmative answer to the question examined. Keep in mind that when using a statistical method for calculating the similarity (e.g. a correlation metric), you will end up with not just the similarity value, but also with a p-value corresponding to it. Although this is usually small, it is something that you may want to consider in your analysis.

It is good to have in mind that whatever results your tests yield, they are not fool-proof. Regardless of whether they pass a statistical significance test or not, it is still possible that the conclusion is not correct. While the chances of this happening are small (the p-value is a good indicator for this), it is good to remember that so that you maintain a sense of humility regarding your conclusions and you are not taken by surprise if the unexpected occurs.

Finally, it is sometimes the case that we need to carry out additional iterations in our experiments and even perform new tests to check additional hypotheses. This may seem frustrating, but it is a normal part of the process, and to some degree expected in data science work. If by the end of the experiments, you end up with a larger number of questions than answers to your original ones, that's fine. This is just how science works in the real world!

Summary

Experiments are essential in checking a hypothesis in a scientific manner and gaining a better understanding of the dynamics of the variables examined. When it comes to simple questions that have clear-cut hypotheses, experiments take the form of a statistical test. The most common tests in data science are the t-test (continuous variables) and the chi-square test (discrete variables).

Although many experiments involve a statistical test on your data directly, often they require more work, such as when you need to assess the performance of a predictive analytics model. In this case, you need to perform a number of runs of your model, calculate a performance metric or two, and perform some statistical analysis in the aggregate of this metric's values, usually through a t-test or something equivalent. K-fold cross validation is a popular method for sampling the data in these kinds of experiments and allows for more robust results.

Confidence in the statistical analysis of results, be it from a straight-forward statistical test or from the testing of the outputs of a simulation, is important. This is usually expressed as a probability value (p-value) and its relationship to a predefined threshold. The lower the p-value in a test, the higher the confidence of the result, which relates to the disproving of the null hypothesis in favor of the alternative hypothesis.

Evaluating the results of an experiment is done through the confidence measure of the tests performed, its comparison with a given threshold, as well as with the use of sensitivity analysis of the conclusion drawn.

Sensitivity Analysis of Experiment Conclusions

Experiment conclusions may be convincing, but this does not make them immune to instability, especially if they stem from a small or a somewhat unrepresentative dataset. To tackle this fairly serious matter, we employ a particular method called *sensitivity analysis*, a practice common to all scientific experiments, but not particularly common to data science. In this chapter, we will look at why it is very important in our field, how it is related to the well-known butterfly effect, the most common ways of performing sensitivity analysis using resampling, and how "what if" questions fit into all of this.

The Importance of Sensitivity Analysis

No matter how well we design and conduct our experiments, there is always some bias there, be it in the data we use, the implicit assumptions, or in how we analyze the results and draw the conclusions of these processes. Unfortunately, this bias is a kind of mistake that often goes by unnoticed, and unless we are aware of this issue and take action, our conclusions may not hold true in the future.

Imagine that you created a model based on the answers of certain questions about the data at hand, only to find out that these answers were not as reliable as they seemed. You probably would not want to put such a model into production!

These issues and uncertainties that may threaten the trustworthiness of your work are bound to disappear with just a bit of extra validation work in the form of sensitivity analysis. As a bonus, such a process is likely going to provide you with additional understanding of the experiments analyzed and help you gain deeper insight into the dynamics of the data you have. The fact that many people don't use sensitivity analysis techniques because they don't know much about it should not be a reason for you to avoid it too.

There are two broad categories of techniques you can use for sensitivity analysis depending on the scope of the analysis: *global* and *local*. We will look into each one of these later on in this chapter. Before we do so, let's take a look at a very interesting phenomenon called the butterfly effect, which captures the essence of the dynamics of such systems that need sensitivity analysis in the first place.

The Butterfly Effect

This is probably one of the most easily recognizable terms of modern science, with various versions of it present in pop culture (particularly films). Unfortunately, its interpretations in the non-scientific media may lead you to believe that it is something very niche, akin to the sophisticated field of science from which it came: Chaos Theory. However, even though it became known to scientists through the study of complex systems (e.g. the weather, the stock market, and anything with behavior that is too chaotic to predict accurately), the butterfly effect is present in many places, including data science experiments.

In essence, the butterfly effect entails a noticeable change in the result stemming from a minute change in the initial conditions of a simulation. It came about in weather prediction models in the early days of computers, when a researcher noticed that the same inputs in a model resulted in entirely different results. After some investigation, it turned out the initial inputs were slightly different (some rounding had taken place), and this small difference was gradually magnified in the time-series model for the weather forecast until it became evident in the later predictions of it.

The butterfly effect makes its appearance in data science experiments usually when a change in the sample alters the conclusions of the tests performed on it. It may also appear in cases of models when there is a set of parameters they rely on. Whatever the case, it isn't something good, especially if you plan to act on the conclusions of your experiments for the development of your data analytics models.

Global Sensitivity Analysis Using Resampling Methods

One popular and effective way of tackling the inherent uncertainty of experimental results in a holistic manner is *resampling methods* (there are other methods for global sensitivity analysis, but these are beyond the scope of this book, as they are not as popular). Resampling methods are a set of techniques designed to provide a more robust way of deriving reliable conclusions from a dataset by trying out different samples of the dataset (which is also a sample of sorts). Although this methodology has been traditionally statistics-based, since the development of efficient simulation processes, it has come to include different ways of accomplishing that too. Apart from purely statistical methods for resampling, such as *bootstrapping, permutation methods,* and *jackknife*, there is also *Monte Carlo* (a very popular method in all kinds of approximation problems). Let's look at each category in more detail.

Bootstrapping

Also known as the Bootstrap method, this resampling technique attempts to do something seemingly impossible. Namely, it tries to gain more information about the population of the data of the sample, using the same sample, much like trying to elevate yourself by lifting the straps of the boots you are wearing (hence the method's peculiar name).

Although additional samples independent of the original one would clearly provide more information about the population, a single sample can also accomplish this. Bootstrapping manages this by randomly selecting sub-samples of the original sample *with replacement*. Given a large enough number of sub-samples (at least 10,000), it is possible to generate a reliable confidence interval of the metric we wish to measure (e.g. the p-value of a t-test). This allows us to see if the value of the metric in the original sample is stable or not, something that no statistical test could tell us beforehand. Naturally, the larger the range of the confidence interval, the more unstable the particular metric is.

Permutation Methods

Permutation methods are a clever way to perform resampling while making sure that the resulting samples are different from one another, much like the bootstrapping method. The main differences are that in the case of permutation methods, the sampling is *without replacement*. Additionally, the process aims to test against hypotheses of "no effect" rather than find confidence intervals of a metric. The number of permutations possible is limited, since no two sub-samples should be the same. However, as the number of data points in each sub-sample is fairly small compared to the number of data points in the original sample, the number of possible permutations is very high. As for the number of sub-samples needed, having around 10,000 sub-samples is plenty for all practical purposes.

Permutation methods are also known as the randomization technique and it is very established as a resampling approach. Also, it is important to note that this set of methods is assumption-free. Regardless of the distribution of the metrics we calculate (e.g. the p-value of a t-test), the results of this meta-analysis are guaranteed to be reliable.

Jackknife

Jackknife is a lesser-known method that offers an alternative way to perform resampling, different than the previous ones, as it focuses on estimating the bias and the standard error of a particular metric (e.g. the median of a variable in the original sample). Using a moderate amount of calculations (more than the previous resampling methods), it systematically calculates the required metric by leaving a single data point out of the original sample in each calculation of the metric.

Although this method may seem time-consuming in the case of a fairly large original sample, it is very robust and allows you to gain a thorough understanding of your data and its sensitivity to the metric you are interested in. If you delve deeper into this approach, you can pinpoint the specific data points that influence this metric. For the purpose of analyzing data stemming from an experiment, it is highly suitable, since it is rare that you will have an exceedingly large amount of data points in this kind of data.

Monte Carlo

This is a fairly popular method for all kinds of approximations, particularly the more complex ones. It is used widely for simulations of the behavior of complicated processes and is very efficient due to its simplicity and ease of use.

When it comes to resampling, Monte Carlo is applied as the following process:

1. Create a simulated sample using a non-biased randomizing method. This sample is based on the population whose behavior you plan to investigate.
2. Create a pseudo-sample emulating a real-life sample of interest (in our case, this can be a predictive model or a test for a question we are attempting to answer)
3. Repeat step 2 for a total of N times
4. Compute the probability of interest from the aggregate of all the outcomes of the N trials from steps 2 and 3

From this meta-testing, we obtain a rigorous insight regarding the stability of the conclusions of our previous experiments, expressed as a p-value, just like the statistical tests we saw in the previous chapter.

Local Sensitivity Analysis Employing "What If?" Questions

"What If?" questions are great, even if they do not lend themselves directly to data-related topics. However, they have a place in sensitivity analysis, as they can prove valuable in testing the stability of a conclusion and how specific parameters relate to this. Namely, such a question can be something like, "What if parameter X increases by 10%? How does this affect the model?" Note that these parameters often relate to specific features, so these questions are also meaningful to the people not directly involved in the model (e.g. the stakeholders of the project).

The high-level comprehensiveness of this approach is one of its key advantages. Also, as this approach involves the analysis of different scenarios, it is often referred to as scenario analysis and is common in even non-data science related situations. Finally, they allow you to delve deeper into the data and the models that are based on it, oftentimes yielding additional insights to complement the ones stemming from your other analyses.

Some Useful Considerations on Sensitivity Analysis

Although sensitivity analysis is more of a process that can help us decide how stable a model is or how robust the answers to your questions are, it is also something that can be measured. However, in practice we rarely put a numeric value to it, mainly because there are more urgent matters that demand our time. Besides, in the case of a model, whatever model we decide on will likely be updated or even replaced altogether by another model, so even if it is not the most stable model in the world, that's acceptable.

However, if you are new to this and find that you have the time to delve deeper into sensitivity analysis when evaluating the robustness of a model, you can calculate the *sensitivity metric*, an interesting heuristic that reflects how sensitive a model is to a particular parameter (we will look into heuristics more in Chapter 11). You can accomplish this as follows:

1. Calculate the relative change of a parameter X
2. Record the corresponding change in the model's performance
3. Calculate the relative change of the model's performance
4. Divide the outcome of step 3 by the outcome of step 1

The resulting number is the sensitivity corresponding to parameter X. The higher it is, the more sensitive (i.e. dependent) the model's performance is to that parameter.

In the previous chapter, we examined K-fold cross validation briefly. This method is actually a very robust way to tackle instability issues proactively, since it reduces the risk of having a good performance in a model due to chance in the sample used to train it. However, the chance of having a lucky streak in sampling is not eliminated completely, which is why in order to ensure that you have a truly well-performing model, you need to repeat the K-fold cross validation a few times.

Playing around with sensitivity analysis is always useful, even if you are an experienced data scientist. The fact that many professionals in this fields choose not to delve too much into it does not make it any less valuable. Especially in the beginning of your data science career, sensitivity analysis can help you to better comprehend the models and understand how relative the answers to your questions are once they are tested with data-based experiments. Even if a test clears an answer for a given question on your data, keep in mind that the answer you obtained may not always hold true, especially if the sample you have is unrepresentative of the whole population of the variables you work with.

Summary

Sensitivity analysis is a rigorous way to check if the conclusions of an experiment are stable enough to be reliable.

The butterfly effect is a term denoting the potential large effects of minor changes in the initial conditions of an experiment. This phenomenon is something very practical in everyday situations when it comes to data science problems, as it manifests in many experiments and data analytics models.

Resampling methods are a popular and effective way to perform sensitivity analysis for a particular test on the data at hand without needing additional data. Resampling methods include bootstrapping, permutation methods, Jackknife, and Monte Carlo.

"What if" questions are useful for sensitivity analysis, as they allow for pinpointing how specific changes in the data are influencing the end result.

PART 3

Common Errors in Data Science

CHAPTER 8

Programming Bugs

Programming bugs are every coder's nightmare, and since data science is intimately connected to coding, they are also every data scientist's nightmare. This is because real data science (i.e. the data science done in the real world and in research centers of most universities) involves a lot of coding. Perhaps some data scientists can get by using a few off-the-shelf methods, but with automation becoming more and more widespread, it is doubtful these people will be adding real value for much longer. In other words, if you want to remain relevant in the data science field, getting your hands dirty with coding is a requirement, not a matter of choice. And wherever there is coding, there are programming bugs. You may be able to resolve some of them through some searching on the web, but unfortunately, many of these coding issues require additional work.

In this chapter, we will explore the most common areas where bugs creep up and the different types of bugs that you are bound to encounter. We will examine how you can tackle these issues and what we can learn from them to improve our craft.

The Importance of Understanding and Dealing with Programming Bugs

With all the talk about AI these days and how it is revamping the data science field, you may be tempted to think it is going to solve all of your problems. However, even if AI makes things easier and more efficient, it cannot change the fact that bugs and human errors are still going to be around (unless of course the whole process is outsourced to AI, something we will discuss in the last part of this book). If you believe that AI is going to do away with all your programming problems, you may want to reconsider your viewpoint!

It is good to keep in mind that even the most adept data scientists have bugs in their code from time to time. Being more experienced may allow you to come up with solutions faster, and the quality of these solutions is bound to be higher than that of a newcomer. However, experience will not get rid of all your mistakes when writing code, since many of these mistakes are due to factors beyond your control (such as fatigue and having too many things on your mind). Therefore, coming up with a robust strategy for dealing with these problems is going to be useful, if not essential, for many years to come.

Bugs are not always bad. If you look past the frustration they cause, they can be the source of useful lessons, especially in the early stages of your career. Examining them closely and tackling them with the right attitude can be a great way to learn more about the programming language you are using, the algorithms implemented, and how all of this fits into the data science pipeline. Let's look into this in more detail, starting with the places where bugs tend to appear.

Places You Usually Find Bugs

Looking at the various places where you are more likely to encounter bugs in your code is an important endeavor, as it is bound to help you classify these bugs and gradually gain a better understanding of your strengths and weaknesses when it comes to the coding aspect of your work as a data scientist. This is especially useful when you are new to coding and wish to improve your skills quickly.

A place where bugs often flock is variables, particularly when you are new to the programming language. Fortunately, most high-level languages such as Julia and Python are able to adapt the variables' types so that they are best suited for the values assigned to them in your code. Still, it is not uncommon, even when using such languages, to make mistakes with how you use these variables, leading to exceptions and errors in your scripts. You will always need to be conscious of how you handle variables when you are programming.

Coding structures, such as conditional statements and loops, can also be a nest for bugs. These bugs may be subtle and are equally vexing and can sometimes be seriously problematic, since they do not always throw errors when you run the scripts that contain bugs like this.

Functions are complex structures, and as such, they deserve lots of attention. Specifically in modern programming languages such as Scala and Julia where they play a more important role, functions tend to be a place where bugs creep up. This is even if these functions are tested individually and work fine in the majority of cases they are tested on.

An even more subtle kind of buggy situation appears whenever there are issues with your code's logic. This is the most difficult situation you will encounter, as bugs in the area of a code's logic are far more elusive and tend to remain unnoticed until they create issues.

Finally, a bug may come out in a combination of the aforementioned places. Bugs like that are even more challenging to resolve, but may give you valuable insight about the inner workings of the code you use. Now let's look at the different types of bugs more closely.

Types of Bugs Commonly Encountered

Much like the bugs found in nature, coding bugs vary greatly, with some of them being more frustrating than others. Yet all of them can be dealt with if you understand them properly and learn to identify them when they creep up in your scripts.

First, we have the bugs which are fairly simple and relatively easy to tackle. These bugs have to do with the *type* of a variable. Since most modern languages are forgiving when it comes to variable types, it is easy to fall into the habit of not paying attention to them. Most data scientists do not particularly care about programming, to the extent people training in that skill do, so it is often the case that types are not set properly, resulting in various issues with the corresponding variables. Best case scenario, you lose some of the accuracy of the variables that should have been defined as Floats but were defined as Integers. Worst case scenario, the problem with the variable types gets unnoticed and creates issues later on. If the compiler of the language identifies such a problem and throws an exception or an error, it should be a cause of celebration, since at least in that case, you become instantly aware of the issue and you can remedy it before it causes other, subtler bugs later on in the program.

Indexing bugs are also fairly common, especially if you are uncertain about the dimensionality of the arrays you are trying to access. Sometimes the language you use may not be able to accept binary arrays as indexes, resulting in errors. Other times, you may be using a different indexing paradigm than the one the language is designed with. For example, the indexes in Julia as well as in R always start with 1, unlike other, more traditional languages, such as Python and C, that start with 0. Also, these languages have a different last element in their arrays than you might expect. For example, a 20 x 1 array in Python (let's call it A) has indexes ranging from 0 to 19, so trying to access element A[20] will yield an error. To access the last element, you will need to refer to it is as A[19] or A[-1]. Moreover, even though negative indexes are acceptable in Python, other languages may not understand them and will throw an error when you attempt to use them.

Parameter value issues are another type of bug closer to home when it comes to data science applications. Sometimes these values are not set right, resulting in issues with the functions they correspond to. These issues are not always easy to detect since they do not always translate to errors, so it is best to make sure that whenever you are setting a value for a parameter, you know what values you should choose from for the function to work in a meaningful way. Otherwise, you may end up with results that don't make much sense or compromise the effectiveness of your models.

Another type of bug has to do with code that never runs (or runs so infrequently that you never get to test it properly under normal circumstances). This is due to the existence of conditionals that are peculiar in the sense that one or more of the conditions present may never (or very rarely) hold true, resulting in whole branches of your code remaining dormant. The code may look fine (i.e. be void of obvious bugs), but may not always yield the results you expect. Unfortunately, a compiler is not sophisticated enough to detect this kind of bug, and the issues they may cause are bound to surface after a long time, possibly after you are done with that part of the project. This can result in delays in your project (if you are fortunate), though it is quite possible that the issues may be much worse (e.g. problematic situations arising when the script is already in production).

Sometimes, conditionals may result in infinite loops, which are yet another type of bug. These bugs are generally easier to pinpoint, though not any less vexing than the other bugs mentioned in this chapter. Note that infinite loops can be very expensive when it comes to the computing resources they consume, so you need to be careful with this kind of bug. Also, since many scripts take a while to run, especially when you are testing them on a single computer, infinite loops may not be apparent and you may waste not just your computing resources, but a lot of time too (waiting for the script to finish running).

It is good to keep in mind that oftentimes the outputs of a function are diverse, depending on the inputs or on other factors (a common situation when dealing with languages supporting *multiple dispatch*). Even though in the vast majority of cases a function yields a certain kind of output, it is possible for it to yield a completely different one that may mess up your code if you have not accounted for that possibility. This type of bug is also subtle, so it will not be identified by the compiler. Instead, when the problem arises, the computer is bound to make sure you become aware of this kind of bug by yielding the corresponding error.

There are also other types of bugs beyond these ones. These other types are more application-specific, and because of this, it is hard to talk about them in any meaningful way. However, they exist, so it is best to be mindful of your code. Things can get very complex and fast as you build more and more scripts that rely on other scripts. Even if the individual pieces of code appear to be simple enough to be bug-free, sometimes just the sheer amount of code you need to run will generate problems you had not anticipated. Therefore, it is advised that you expect this and always budget time for it. This way, when the time comes to debug these scripts, you can do so without getting stressed out.

Some Useful Considerations on Programming Bugs

Although programming bugs are generally a cause for delays and vexing situations, they are part of the package and are what make the scripts valuable, in a way. If everyone could write a program easily and without any issues, no-one would want to pay someone to do it and do it well. Avoiding programming is not a solution though, since it is programming that most empowers data science. It is unlikely that you will be able to do much in the field of data science without writing some code. Also, data science algorithms are always evolving. Even if you can perform some processes without having to write your own scripts, chances are that sooner or later you will need to do some coding if you want to remain relevant as a data scientist.

Handling bugs is a skill that you gradually develop. Although it is unlikely that your code-writing will ever be completely void of bugs, if you pay close attention to your programming mistakes, you will be able to limit them. As a bonus, this kind of experience can enable you to be a good communicator of the programming mindset and a great troubleshooter, essential skills in all mentoring endeavors. Hopefully the information in this chapter will enable you to pinpoint and understand the bugs in your programs and gradually come to accept them as issues that need to be tackled, just like problematic data or obscure requirements.

Summary

Programming bugs are a frustrating, yet inevitable situation a data scientist encounters. However, with the right attitude, they can also be useful lessons in terms of the programming language used, the algorithms involved, and the data science pipeline overall.

AI cannot rid the data science domain of bugs altogether.

Programming bugs are typically encountered in the following areas:

- **Variable types**. These involve using the wrong type in a variable
- **Coding structures**. These are subtle issues that involve more elaborate aspects of coding, such as loops
- **Functions**. This is particularly important in cases where the same function is used in different programs, as is often the case in modern programming languages
- **Logic of the code**. Bugs in this area are harder to pinpoint, as they involve issues with the algorithm behind the code

The types of bugs that are most often encountered in data science scripts are the following:

- **Simple ones**, such as those related to variable types
- **Indexing bugs**, involving access to arrays, be it vectors, matrices, or multi-dimensional data structures
- **Bugs related to parameter values**. Most subtle bugs involving the input of a function, such as inputting a value that is out of range or problematic when in combination with other parameter values
- **Code that never runs, or runs very rarely**. A side-effect of conditionals where there is insufficient forethought about the various possibilities they cover
- **Infinite loops**. Bugs that have to do with loops that never terminate, wasting computer resources and your time
- **Bugs having to do with the output of a function**. When the output of a function is not what you expect and you feed it to some other function or to a model
- **Other bug types**. Bugs that are specific to a particular application or framework, beyond the cases covered in this list

CHAPTER 9

Mistakes Through the Data Science Process

Mistakes are inevitable, not just in coding as we saw in the previous chapter, but also through the whole data science pipeline. This is more or less obvious. What is not obvious is that these mistakes are also learning opportunities for you, and that no matter how experienced you are, they are bound to creep up on you. Naturally, the better your grasp of data science, the lower your chances of making these mistakes, but as the field constantly changes, it is likely that you will not be on top of every aspect of it.

In this chapter, we will examine the difference between mistakes and bugs, the most common types of mistakes in data science, how the selection of a model can be erroneous (even if it does not create apparent issues that will make you identify it as a mistake), the value of a mentor in discovering these mistakes, and additional considerations about mistakes in the data science process.

How Mistakes Differ From Bugs

Although bugs are mistakes of sorts, the mistakes in the data science process are of higher-level and more challenging to deal with overall. In particular, they have to do with either some misunderstanding of the pipeline or some general issues with how it is applied to a particular problem. The main issue with mistakes is that because they are high-level, they do not typically yield errors or exceptions, so they are easy to neglect, creating issues in the end-result of your project, whether that is in the data product or the insights.

As I discussed in the first part of the book, the data science pipeline can be time-consuming, as new ideas often come up as you go through it. This urges you to go back to previous steps and revisit your feature set, making a certain amount of back-and-forths inevitable. However, a simple mistake can force you into more back-and-forths in your process, causing additional delays. Being able to limit these mistakes can significantly improve your efficiency and the quality of your insights, as you will have more time to spend on meaningful tasks rather than troubleshooting issues you could have avoided.

Still, as you progress in your career as a data scientist, the mistakes you make are bound to become more and more subtle (and as a result, more interesting). Some bystanders may even not recognize them as mistakes, which is why those mistakes tend to require more effort and commitment to excellence to remedy them. One thing is for certain: mistakes will never vanish completely. Also, the sooner you realize that they are part of the daily life of a data scientist, the more realistic your expectations about your work and the field in general. With the right attitude, you can turn these mistakes into opportunities for growth that will make you a better data scientist and transform this otherwise vexing process of discovering and amending into priceless lessons.

Most Common Types of Mistakes

Let us now take a look at the most common types of mistakes in the data science process that people in the field tend to make, particularly in the early part of their careers. Even if your scripts are entirely bug-free, you may still fall victim to subtle errors which can oftentimes be more challenging than the simpler issues with the code you write.

The majority of the data science process mistakes involve the data engineering part of the pipeline – data cleaning in particular. A lot of data science practitioners nowadays are fond of data modeling and tend to forget that for the models to function well, the data that is fed into them has to be prepared properly. This takes place in the data engineering stage, an essential and time-consuming part of the pipeline. However, data cleaning has to do with more than merely getting rid of corrupt data and formatting the remaining parts of the raw data so that it forms a dataset. If there are a lot of missing values, we may have to examine these data points and see how they relate to the rest of the dataset, especially the target variables when we are dealing with a prediction analytics problem. Moreover, sometimes the arithmetic mean is not the right metric to use when replacing these missing values with something else. Plus, when it comes to classification problems, we need to take into account the class structure of the dataset before replacing these missing values. If you neglect any one of these steps, you are bound to distort the signal of the dataset, which is a costly mistake in this part of the pipeline.

The process of feature creation is an integral part of the data science pipeline, especially if the data at hand does not lend itself to advanced data analytics methods. Feature creation is not an easy task. The majority of beginners in the data science field find it very challenging and tend to neglect it. On the bright side, the programming part of it is fairly straight-forward, so if you are confident in your programming skills, it is unlikely to yield any bugs. Also, if you pay attention to the feature creation stage, you will likely save a lot of time later on, while at the same time get better results in your models. The mistakes data scientists make in this stage are usually not related to the feature creation per se, but rather to the fact that the time they dedicate in this process is insufficient. Coming up with new features is not the same as feature extraction, an often automated process for condensing the feature set into a set of meta-features (also known as super-features). Creating new features, even if many of them end unused, is useful in that it allows you to get to know the data on a deeper level through a creative process. Moreover, the new features you select from the ones you have come up with are bound to be useful additions to the existing features, making the parts of your project that follow considerably easier.

Issues related to sampling are not as common, but they are still a type of mistake you can encounter in your data science endeavors. Naturally, sampling a dataset properly (i.e. with random sampling) that does not have any measurable biases is essential for training and testing your models. This is why we often need to use several samples to ensure our models are stable, as we briefly saw in Chapter 7. Using a single or a small number of samples will usually bring about models that do not have adequate generalization. Therefore, not paying attention to this process when building your models is a serious mistake that can throw off even the most promising models you create.

As we saw in a previous chapter, model evaluation is an important part of the data science pipeline related to the model development stage. Nevertheless, it often does not get the necessary attention, and many people rush to use their models without spending enough time evaluating them. Model evaluation is essential for making sure that there are no biases present, a process that is often handled through K-fold cross validation as we have seen. Yet using this method only a single time is rarely enough. Therefore, the conclusions drawn from an insufficient analysis of the model can easily be a liability, particularly if that model is chosen to go into production afterwards. All of this constitutes a serious mistake that is unfortunately all too common among those unaware of the value of sampling.

Over-fitting a model is another issue that comes about from a superficial approach to the data modeling stage and which constitutes another important mistake. This is closely linked to the previous issues, as it involves the performance of models. Specifically, it has to do with models performing well for some data but horribly for most other data. In other words, the model is too specialized and its generalization is insufficient for it to be broadly useful. Allowing over-fitting in a model is a serious mistake which can put the whole project at risk if it is not handled properly.

Another mistake deals with the assumptions behind the tests we do or the metrics we calculate. Sometimes, these assumptions do not apply to the data at hand, making the conclusions that stem from them less robust then we may think and subject to change if the underlying discrepancies are stretched further. For most tests performed in everyday data science, this is a common but not a crucial problem (e.g. the t-test can handle many cases where the assumptions behind it are not met, without yielding misleading results). Since some cases are more sensitive than others, when it comes to their assumptions, it is best to be aware of this issue and avoid it whenever possible.

Finally, there are other types of mistakes which are not related to the above types, as they are more application-specific (e.g. mistakes related to the architectural design of an AI system or to the modeling of an NLP problem). I will not go into any detail about them here, but I recommend that you are aware of them, since all the mistakes mentioned here are merely the tip of the iceberg. The data science process may be simple enough to understand and apply effectively, but it entails many complications, and every aspect of it requires considerable attention. The more mindful you are about the data pipeline, the less likely you are to make any mistakes which can cause delays or other issues with your data science projects.

Choosing the Right Model

Choosing the right model for a given problem is often the root of a fundamental mistake in data science that tends to go unnoticed, which is why I dedicate a section to it. This is linked to understanding the problem you are trying to solve and figuring out the best strategy to move forward. There are a variety of models out there that can work with your data, but that does not mean that they are suitable as potential solutions to the data modeling part of the pipeline.

What is the right model anyway? More often than not, there is no single model that is optimum for your data, which is why you need to try several models before you make a choice. Take into account a variety of factors that are relevant to your project. This is how you decide on the model you plan to utilize and eventually put it into production. All of this can be challenging, especially if you are new to the organization. The most common related scenarios which can constitute different manifestations of the model-selection mistake are the following:

- **Choosing a model just because it is supposed to be good or popular in the data science community**. This is the most common mistake related to model selection. Although there is nothing wrong with the models presented in articles or the models used by the "experts," it is often the case that they are not the best ones to choose for every situation. The right model for a particular problem depends on various factors, and it is virtually impossible to know which one it would be beforehand. So, going for an expert's a priori view on what should work would be unscientific and imprudent.

- **Selecting a model because it has a very high accuracy rate**. This kind of model-related mistake is more subtle. Although accuracy is important when it comes to predictive analytics problems, it is not always the best evaluation metric to rely on. Sometimes the nature of the problem calls for a very specific kind of performance metric, such as the F1 metric, or perhaps a model that is easy to interpret or implement. There is also the case that speed is of utmost importance, so a faster model is preferred to a super-accurate one.

- **Going for a model because it is easy to understand and work with**. This is a typical rookie mistake, but it can happen to data sciences pros as well. If models are overly simple and have a ton of literature on them, some data scientists go for them, as they lack the discernment to make a more informed decision. Models like that may be easy to defend as well, since everyone in a data analytics division has heard of a statistical inference system, for example.

- **Deciding on a model because it is faster than every other option you have**. Having a fast model to train and use is great, but in many cases, this is not enough to make it the optimum choice. It is worth it to consider a more time-consuming model that can guarantee a higher value in terms of accuracy rate or F1 metric. So, choosing a model for its speed may not be a great option, unless speed is one of the key requirements of the systems you plan to deploy.

Dealing with each one of these possibilities will not only help you avoid a mistake related to the data modeling stage, but also increase your confidence in the model you end up selecting.

Value of a Mentor

Having a mentor in your life, especially in the beginning of your career, is a priceless resource. Not only will he be able to help you with general career advice, but he can answer questions you may have about specific technical topics, such as methodological matters in the data science pipeline. In fact, a mentor would probably be your best source of information about these matters, especially if it is someone who is active in the field and has hands-on knowledge of the craft.

It is important to have specific topics to discuss with your mentor in order to make the most of your time with them. What's more, he may be able to help you develop a positive approach to dealing with the mistakes you make and enable you to go deeper into the ideas behind each one of them. This will also help you develop a holistic understanding of data science and its pipeline.

Some Useful Considerations on Mistakes

Mistakes in the data science process are not something to be ashamed of or to conceal. In fact, mistakes are worth discussing with other people in the field, especially more knowledgeable ones. They provide opportunities to delve into what you need to learn the most. No one is perfect, and even things that are considered good in data science now may prove to be sub-optimal or even bad in the future. So, if you start feeling complacent about your work, this may be a sign that you are not putting in enough effort. Data science is not an exact science, and the solutions that may be acceptable for now may not be good enough in the future. Keeping that in mind will help you avoid all kinds of issues throughout your data science career.

Allowing your thinking of the data science process to become stagnant is possibly the worst kind of mistake a person can make in this field, as data science greatly depends on having a flow of ideas, driven by creativity and evaluated by experimentation.

Summary

Mistakes in the data science process are inevitable, but they can be educational, particularly for newcomers in the field. Mistakes are different from programming bugs, as they tend to be more high-level, methodological, and harder to pinpoint.

The most common types of mistakes in the data science process are related to one or more of the following areas:

- Data engineering, particularly data cleansing
- Feature creation
- Sampling
- Model evaluation
- Over-fitting
- Not adhering to the assumptions behind a test or a process

Choosing the right model for a data science project is a process that requires special attention. The main mistakes related to this process are:

- Selecting a model merely because it is supposed to be good or it is popular among data scientists
- Using accuracy as the sole determinant of model-selection
- Deciding on a model because it is easier to understand than the other options
- Using speed as the only criterion for model-selection

A mentor can be a great asset in figuring out potential mistakes in the data science process and resolving them effectively, while at the same time learning about the ideas behind them.

CHAPTER 10

Handling Bugs and Mistakes

Once you have identified bugs in your code or mistakes in the data science process, you need to deal with them in an effective and efficient manner. In this chapter, I will examine how you can accomplish this so that you do not need to dedicate too many resources on these often annoying situations. In addition, I will discuss some ideas for selecting the most appropriate model in order to prevent the more serious pipeline issues as much as possible.

Strategies for Coping with Bugs

As we saw in Chapter 8, bugs can be a major inconvenience. Still, they are very difficult to avoid. So, in order to cope with this matter and not let it disrupt your workflow, it is essential to come up with various strategies to deal with bugs or even prevent them altogether. Let's look at some such strategies that have been shown to be an effective practice in this regard.

A somewhat controversial-sounding strategy that is nevertheless guaranteed to take care of some bugs is using static-typed functions in all of your programs. This will enable you to be on top of all the type issues that often plague scripts, and therefore eliminate the possibility of such a bug arising. If there is a type mismatch, it will become evident early, making it easy to deal with before it wastes much of your time. Also, this will give your code performance boost, at least in certain programming languages, such as Julia. If you are using Python, you can use a package called *mypy* for checking the types of your scripts to see if they are properly defined. Moreover, you can make use of hints in your code to ensure that later users of these functions know what types are supposed to go into them and what types are expected to come out in the outputs.

In addition, you can take care of many potential bugs proactively by setting up a series of unit tests. These are QA tests focused on making sure your scripts work as they are expected to by covering a large variety of inputs and potential outputs, ensuring that the scripts are void of bugs that can manifest under normal operating circumstances. This is the most essential kind of quality control you can do on your code, and it is common as a practice among both coders as well as the more technically adept data scientists.

Another strategy that may seem apparent to most people in this field has to do with how you test a data analytics script you have written against data. It is best to start small, meaning that instead of running your code on the whole dataset, use only a small sample of it. This will ensure that it does not hang or yield nonsensical results within a reasonable amount of time. This last part is highly important, as your code needs to be able to scale well, otherwise it may not be usable. This simple strategy will save you time in general and reveal issues the script may have more quickly, as you will be able to customize its input to cover a large number of possibilities.

Also, a strategy that is common among programmers and which applies well to data science professionals too, is sharing your scripts with other people in the field whom you trust, especially people you already work with, as they are bound to be more directly impacted by your code. In case you have a mentor, it would be a good idea to show them your script as well, in order to obtain additional feedback and valuable guidance. It is useful to keep in mind that you are not on your own, no matter how self-sufficient you may feel. Beyond the debugging part, sharing your code with others can even bring about insight on how you can optimize it.

Finally, a popular practice which stems from sharing your code is called pair-coding. This has to do with coding together with another person as a team. Usually one of you sits and does the scripting, while the other drives the process through pitching ideas and observing all that is being done to ensure the code makes sense. As you might expect, the roles in the project change periodically, so parties working on the project will get a more holistic experience of the process. Pair-coding is helpful particularly if you are new to programming; apart from pinpointing your programming issues and inefficiencies, it also helps you build confidence in your coding skills over time.

Strategies for Coping with High-level Mistakes

As we saw in the previous chapter, high-level mistakes, such as those related to the data science pipeline, can be challenging and time-consuming to deal with, even more than with programming bugs. Luckily, there are effective strategies for dealing even with these kinds of mistakes.

First of all, you can pick a data science case study, perhaps even a solved problem, and study it, focusing on how it follows the various stages of the pipeline. Even if all the steps are familiar to you, there is still a lot you can learn from this drill. Moreover, by studying this material carefully, you can gradually hone your intuition about what needs to be done and how. All of this can help reduce the number of mistakes you make through the data science process.

Another strategy you can employ, which is also quite common, is keeping a record of your work and your assumptions through proper documentation. This way, you can always go back to your notes if something goes wrong to figure out why it went wrong. Your notes may also provide you with insight as to how you can remedy the mistakes you may make, saving you energy and time. For instance, maybe an assumption you made did not apply, or you forgot a step in the previous stages. Your documentation will likely be very useful at this stage, not to mention at the end of your project, when you may have to produce a report or a slideshow presentation of your work.

In addition, you can learn more about the data science process through studying it in detail from a reliable source. It would be best to be cautious about amateur material on YouTube though, since there is no quality assurance process in place for anything being published there. For any reliable source you decide on, make sure that you fully comprehend how the data science process applies to different problems, since every application is slightly different.

A strategy that may appear to be more like common sense but is definitely worth mentioning is practice. This is necessary not just for dealing with potential mistakes that you may make in the data science pipeline, but also for cultivating the intuition that will allow you to become efficient at applying the process. As it gradually becomes second nature to you, you will be able to minimize the chances of these mistakes occurring. It may also help you identify mistakes more accurately when they manifest so you can remedy them quicker.

Preventing Erroneous Situations in the Pipeline

As we saw in the previous chapter, choosing the right model is a tricky thing, especially if you are new to the field, making it a potential cause for serious and sometimes hard to identify mistakes in the data science pipeline. This is why we are going to look at this matter more extensively, so that you prevent model selection from becoming an issue that can put your whole project in jeopardy. Here, we will examine the different types of models that are often confused, how data evaluation factors in when it comes to selecting a model, how you can choose among various classification systems, and ensembles' place in all of this.

Types of Models

As we saw in the first part of the book, there are several data science methodologies out there, making the number of potential models fairly large. Most of the issues with choosing the right model have to do with the following methodologies: predictive analytics (e.g. classification vs. regression or classifier A vs. classifier B), anomaly detection (e.g. finding an outlier), exploratory analysis (e.g. clustering) and recommender systems. Your options will not always be narrowed down to a particular category of models, making the process of choosing the right model more challenging.

Of course, there are other model types that are potential options. For example, graph analysis is about relationships among data points in an abstract space that is inherently different than the feature space. If you are asked to predict a particular value of a variable, for example, you are not going to consider graph analysis as an option for a model type.

In the case where you get the model category correct and the data at hand seems to fit to a particular model type, this still does not make every model of that type a viable option. The problem is not as simple as it seems at first. This is why we often need to dig deeper into the data and understand what makes more sense as a model. At the very least, this will point toward the right model category, which is a good start.

Evaluating the Data at Hand and Pairing It with a Model

Evaluating the data available to you is something that goes without saying, yet not everyone thinks of it as a way to figure out the most meaningful model category. However, if you take the time to examine all the data you have, assess each feature's potential for bringing out whatever signals are in the data, and see how it works with the other features, you can gain a much deeper understanding of the problem and what kind of model you can craft. Sometimes it can be something as simple as examining which types of variables in your dataset can hint towards the model category. For example, if you have mainly discrete variables as your target variables, you will need to focus on classification systems, since classification always deals with discrete targets. Also, if you find that you have variables that are full of missing values and that you are looking at finding similar data points, this can point toward a recommender system.

When it comes to exploratory analysis, the one technique that stands out is clustering. This is what you would normally do when you do not have a target variable. Sometimes, you may use the cluster labels as the target variable afterward. There are two distinct possibilities when it comes to performing clustering: either predefine the number of clusters, or let the clustering system work it out. In the first case, you would use something like k-means (or one of its many variants), while in the latter case you would use another system like *DBSCAN*. Keep that in mind so that you do not fall prey to thinking there is only a single option methodology for clustering (revolving around k-means).

Evaluating the data can go deeper, especially if you are knowledgeable about the potential categories of model that are available. For example, if you find that what you are planning to predict is a fairly rare phenomenon that is reflected in a particular variable, you may want to transform that variable to a binary one, with one value being related to all the cases you want to predict, and then seek a model in that anomaly detection domain. Also, if you find that you have several features that loosely relate to a continuous variable you want to predict and find that there is no feature at your disposal that correlates well with the target variable for all of its values, you may want to introduce a discrete variable that acts as an intermediary with the target variable. This way you can use the latter for building a classification model that breaks up the original regression problem into two or more smaller and more manageable problems. Each of these you can tackle using a regression system.

Choosing the Right Model for a Classification Methodology

Classification-related problems are where the biggest confusion comes about. This is mainly because there are so many options to choose from, especially nowadays. Plus, there is a strong trend toward more sophisticated systems that are widely available and well-documented. However, not all problems lend themselves to an advanced classifier that in order to work well, needs a considerable amount of fine-tuning without any guarantee about the stability of the results. Sometimes a simple model is good enough because it is stable and fairly easy to interpret. So, if you are going to be asked about the results afterwards and are expected to know which features are more relevant, for example, and by how much, a black-box classifier would be something best to avoid, while a more transparent system like a random forest or k nearest neighbor (kNN) would be more appropriate. Also, if you find that most of your features are binary and more or less mutually exclusive (i.e. there is very small overlap among them), you may want to consider a Bayesian model.

If it is speed that you are after (at the expense of high accuracy), you may want to go for a basic classification systems like logistic regression or a decision tree, especially if you have done considerable work in feature engineering or if your data is information-rich to start with. Be sure to examine various possibilities when it comes to these systems' hyperparameters, however.

Also, it is important to make sure you are using the right evaluation metrics when choosing the classifier for your project. Perhaps good precision is more important than good recall, while the overall accuracy may be more relevant. Or maybe the different classes are not equally important and it makes more sense to employ a cost function for the misclassifications involved when deciding which classifier is optimal for the problem at hand. Or perhaps the confidence of the classifier is meaningful to you, so you want it to be aligned with the correct classifications, something that is reflected on a good ROC curve. Whatever the case, these are important factors to take into account before benchmarking your classifiers and deciding on the one to rely on in your project.

Combining Different Options in an Ensemble Setting

Sometimes it is the case that the best model option is not a single model but rather a combination of models in the form of an ensemble (see glossary for a definition). In fact, there are a few classification systems which are ensembles under the hood (e.g. random forests and extreme learning machines). The idea is that with an ensemble setting, you attain a better performance (whether this is measured as accuracy rate, F1 score, or some other metric), while at the same time limiting the risk of over-fitting. However, ensembles tend to be more computationally expensive, translating into a lower speed in the classification system. Also, not all classifiers can be merged into an ensemble and have a guaranteed result. In order for the ensemble to be effective, its components are better off being diverse, particularly in terms of the errors they make. This is why the classifiers that comprise them are often trained differently from one another, leading to vastly different generalizations from the same dataset. The differences in training can be because of different data being used (be it different samples or different feature sets), different operational parameters in the classifiers involved, or some combination of both.

Combining different classifiers is not always a simple and straight-forward task. If you are dealing with different classifier types, a simple aggregate function may not be the best way to go, as other factors may need to be taken into account (e.g. the performance of the classifier at a particular region of the data space or its confidence score). Still, with proper attention, ensembles can be a great option to explore, particularly if you find that conventional classification systems fail to deliver a reasonable performance and you are willing to trade speed for performance in your project.

Other Considerations for Choosing the Right Model

There are other things worth considering when choosing the right model for the problem you are tackling. For example, no matter how content you are with your model and how well it performs, its relevancy may change as new data becomes available. That is not to say that suddenly you will need a model from an entirely different category, but most likely you will need to explore other options within the same category (after you try retraining your model to see how it performs with the new data). Also, it may be the case that the requirements of the project change after the model has been in production for a while and there is feedback on its results. For example, in the case of a classification scenario, it could be that the costs involved in the misclassifications have shifted and that a new cost function needs to be implemented (making the current model a suboptimal choice). This is normal, since the world is not a static place and no matter how good a model is, it usually has an expiration date beyond which it is no longer relevant for the particular project.

As your data science expertise grows, you are bound to be able to do more with your data, changing the dynamics of the problem. Perhaps you can now figure out a better synthetic feature that can be used in a model, or filter out noisy data points more effectively, bringing about a more robust feature set. Your new expertise can be a gateway to a better model, which is something that will be worth investigating.

Things are not set in stone in data science. Whether it is because of new data, a new requirement, a new feature you come up with, or some other reason (e.g. another new system becomes available), you need to revisit the models you have selected and either revamp them or replace them altogether.

Summary

Once you have identified the bugs in your code or the mistakes in your data science work, you have to deal with them in an effective manner before they pose a threat to the completion of your project.

You can cope with bugs in various ways, such as:

- Using static-typed functions in all of your scripts
- Performing unit tests on all the programming modules you create
- Running data-related scripts on small samples of your data first
- Sharing code with colleagues and mentors and learning from their feedback
- Doing pair-coding with other data scientists

You can deal with the high-level mistakes in your data science work using various strategies, such as:

- Seeing how the data science pipeline applies to a case study or a solved data science problem of your choice
- Creating documentation of your work, including the assumptions you make throughout the pipeline
- Learning more about the process through studying a reliable source, such as a data science book or video
- Practicing through a data science competition or a problem that lends itself to data science
- Working with a friend on a few data science projects

Choosing the right model is a great way to prevent certain issues in the data science pipeline. This entails the following:

- Recognizing which model or model type the problem is more relevant to by evaluating the data
- Choosing the right system in the classification domain
- Examining the possibility of an ensemble of different models

PART 4

Other Aspects of Data Science

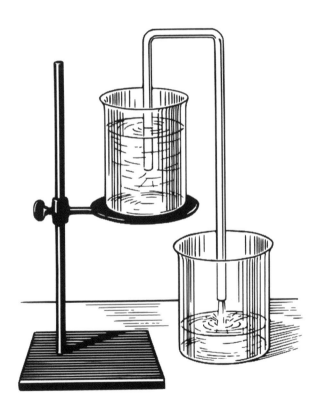

CHAPTER 11

The Role of Heuristics in Data Science

We have mentioned heuristics briefly throughout the book, giving hints that they are an important part of data science. But what are they? In general, a heuristic is a back-of-the-envelope method employed in a computer science system in order to obtain a solution in a fast and inexpensive way.

When it comes to data science, a heuristic takes the form of an empirical metric or function that aims to provide some useful tool or insight, to facilitate a data science method or project. A heuristic can be the source of additional features, or a way to assess the information or value of the data in your models. It is a versatile and invaluable tool in all your data science endeavors.

In this chapter, we will examine heuristics including describing the problems that require heuristics, exploring the importance of heuristics in AI systems and their application in various areas of data science, as well as a view of what makes a heuristic good should you wish to create your own heuristics.

Heuristics as Information in the Making

Heuristics can be thought of as information in the making, even if this information is not so well hidden as that derived from our models. Still, these models often rely on heuristics to a great extent, regardless of if it is not always acknowledged. This is because heuristics are so closely ingrained in computer science that they are often used without bringing about awareness of them. What's more, in the scientific world, they tend to be looked down upon, as there is rarely any scientific theory behind them. That's not to say that heuristics are pseudo-science; they are just more akin to inventions. Although they comply with the laws of science, they may apply science in novel and creative ways, and may even use principles that are not yet thoroughly understood or even studied for that matter. Therefore, heuristics are scientific in essence, even if they are not always well-researched. It is good to remember that something that is a heuristic today may be an application of a scientific theory in the future, despite it being a work in progress right now.

More often than not, a heuristic manifests as an algorithm or a metric. As such, it is responsible for performing some sort of processing or transformation of the data it is given. For example, in the evaluation of a system in the predictive analytics category, it is often the case that heuristics that encapsulate the performance of the system in a single number are used, usually in the [0, 1] interval. More sophisticated heuristics, such as those used in most AI systems, are not that simple and are comprised of a series of steps, in order to apply the concepts behind them. Whatever the case, be it for a simple performance evaluation or for handling the data inside an AI system, heuristics bring out the information residing in the data in a practical and useful way.

In order for heuristics to be as applicable as possible, they need to be fairly simple and easy to scale. This allows them to be efficient in how they use the computational resources available. This is very important, particularly when dealing with large datasets, as is often the case in data science. However, this simplicity can limit them, which is why they are often insufficient in tackling a data analytics problem by themselves. This is also why they are information in the making, but not a complete and refined information product.

Problems that Require Heuristics

Though the majority of problems can be tackled with conventional techniques, there are certain problems where heuristics are essential. This may be due to the complexity of a problem, or because of the restrictions involved (e.g. limited computational resources), as well as other factors, which depend on the domain of the problem.

One of the most common problems in data science and computer science in general is optimization. Even if there are quite a few deterministic methods for finding the optimum value of a function given certain restrictions, usually the problems we need to tackle in the real world have to do with very complex functions that are multi-dimensional and non-linear. This makes calculating the best possible solution extremely difficult, if not practically impossible. Nevertheless, since we do not usually care much about finding the absolute best solution to such problems, we often compromise with solutions that are good enough, as long as we can find them quickly. This prospect is made possible with stochastic optimizers, such as simulated annealing, that rely heavily on heuristics to work.

Problems that involve creativity are particularly tough, making heuristics the only viable alternative. Examples include music composition, artistic drawing, poetry writing, and even the generation of video clips (e.g. movie trailers). For the systems involved in such challenging tasks, heuristics do much of the heavy-lifting in the background. The alternative would be to figure out a mathematical model that describes these processes, something that is yet to emerge.

Going back to data science problems, most likely the models you deal with have a number of parameters, even if the problem you are trying to solve is something fairly simple, such as regression. These parameters often need to be fine-tuned at one point in order for the model to be robust enough (this is particularly true in *deep learning* systems, which are described in more detail in Chapter 12). This fine-tuning often includes selecting the most powerful features through a technique like Lasso or L2 normalization. Methods like these that enable this fine-tuning to take place are basically heuristics embedded in the fitness function of the model.

Classification problems also have much to benefit from heuristics. Oftentimes, we are faced with the challenge that the conventional evaluation metrics, such as *accuracy rate*, fail to measure what we want out of the classifier. Cases like fraud detection and intrusion detection systems are good examples of that. In these cases, accuracy is completely useless, while *F1* can only get us so far. If we want to build a model that is optimal for the problem at hand, we will have to use a custom evaluation system that makes use of a *cost function*. This function is in essence a simple heuristic that makes all of this possible.

Why Heuristics are Essential for an AI System

AI systems continue to thrive due to their seemingly unbounded potential in tackling complex problems and their robust way of utilizing large amounts of data. However, the middle phases where this data is formulated into useful packs of information involve a lot of complex processes that even the creators of these systems are not fully aware of their details. In order to have a firm grasp on this, there are some heuristics in place that are high-level enough to be understood by any user of the system, but also low-level enough to be close to the inner workings of the system (e.g. through the function that conveys the signal between two connected nodes in an *artificial neural network (ANN)*, or *transfer function*).

AI systems rely on heuristics to various extents, depending on the system. All AI systems involve an optimization phase, which is largely heuristics-based (in order for this optimization to be possible in a short enough amount of time). In that sense, any modern AI system would be infeasible without some heuristic working on the back-end. Being highly stochastic in nature, these systems would not be able to learn anything at a reasonable level of generalization if it were not for some heuristic in their training algorithms (optimizing the relevant parameters) or in how these systems are applied afterwards. Otherwise, they would run into all kinds of over-fitting issues, jeopardizing their performance and usefulness in general. However, AI systems also tend to employ an unconventional approach to data analytics, veering away from traditional theory. This enables them to tackle all kinds of datasets without being bound by assumptions related to their distributions, for example. In order to accomplish this, they resort to relying on heuristics, instead of some model of the data that may or may not hold true. More on that in the chapter that follows.

Applications of Heuristics in Data Science

Data science needs heuristics, probably more and more as it evolves into an ever-sophisticated field. The time when we used to tackle structured data stemming from organized data streams is way behind us. These days, the majority of the data we use is highly disorganized, and it is practically impossible to do anything useful with it without heuristics. Especially when it comes to complicated problems, heuristics are essential since such problems often require custom-built evaluation metrics in order to find optimal solutions. Let's look at some of the areas where heuristics can benefit data science.

Heuristics and Machine Learning Processes

Machine learning processes benefit from heuristics a great deal. Be it in the form of evaluation metrics for machine learning models or as components of the models themselves, they can add a lot of value to whatever system you are using. Because heuristics are more helpful in problems that are highly challenging, if your data is fairly clean and tidy and all you care about is the model's overall performance as captured by F1 or accuracy rate, applying heuristics would be an overkill.

Yet, in the cases when the performance you obtain from your models is insufficient or not relevant to what you want in your project, you have a lot to benefit from involving heuristics in the machine learning process. Perhaps a simple heuristic like a custom *cost function* would suffice, or maybe you will need to change the model's inner workings by using a heuristic there (e.g. in the decision-making part, when dealing with a classification system). Whatever the case, machine learning models usually have plenty of room for improvement if you are willing to put the time into employing heuristics.

Custom Heuristics and Data Engineering

Data engineering has also much to benefit from heuristics, perhaps more than any other part of the data science pipeline. This is because this part of the pipeline involves the most tinkering of the data and tends to include a significant amount of out-of-the-box thinking regarding how you can go about improving the morphing of the data at hand into a useful dataset. What is useful is closely related to what is information-rich, and what better way to accomplish that than using flexible data structures and processes that involve information-rich data like heuristics?

For example, you can create custom similarity metrics to establish where two features are alike and by how much (remember, features do not have to be in a linear space, where conventional distance metrics make sense), or to establish the best way to make a continuous feature discrete. By then plugging this heuristic into an optimization system, you can find a good enough discretization of that feature (often referred to as *binning*), such that the information loss is minimal. Similarly, you can use heuristics to merge several discrete features together (feature *fusion*) without having to make use of every possible combination out there. Finally, it is possible (and not too uncommon) to transform a binary feature into a continuous one if we have a binary target variable. This is made possible using a heuristic based on the distribution matrix depicting the four combinations of 1s and 0s of the feature and the target variable.

Heuristics for Feature Evaluation

Feature evaluation in sets is something that most data scientists are unaware is possible, even if its usefulness can be seen almost universally. Also, this methodology is an effective way of performing dimensionality reduction without needing to resort to synthetic features (like those obtained by running PCA or some other SVD method, which is expensive computationally). However, evaluating entire feature sets is only feasible through specialized heuristics designed for this purpose. The alternative is running a model on them, preferably one that you can interpret easily, but this option has the primary drawback that its results are not all that generalizable.

In terms of applied data science, feature evaluation is basically assessing the predictive potential of a set of features. This implies that there is a target variable that is used as a frame reference. Since the only metrics that are supported by theory and that are lightweight enough to be scalable are *correlation coefficient* and *entropy* (as well as variants of it, such as *cross-entropy*), most of the methods for feature evaluation revolve around tackling features one at a time. However, using certain, more modern heuristics (such as one of the *Index of Discernibility* metrics), it is possible to handle whole sets of features at once.

Other Applications of Heuristics

There are also several other applications of heuristics, too many and too application-specific to be included in this chapter. What's more, you can always come up with some of your own, depending on how creative or how much you are in need of them! One application that is worth mentioning is the building of an *ensemble*, a bundle of predictive analytics models that promises to provide a better performance than any one of its components alone.

Many ensemble methods utilize heuristics in some way, particularly in cases when we are dealing with diverse predictive analytics systems as the members of the ensemble. This is because things are not always clear-cut when it comes to combining classifiers or regressors, and even when they are (e.g. in the case of all of the components of the ensemble having a confidence metric accompanying the prediction), this may not be sufficient for combining the outputs of the ensemble members, mainly because the value of these confidence metrics often vary greatly among different systems. So, if you find the use of random forests appealing, but are not satisfied with conventional ensemble options, give heuristics a try to see if you can work out a way to combine different predictive analytics systems in an ensemble setting.

Anatomy of a Good Heuristic

Good heuristics are like good data science educational materials: few and hard to find. As a result, it takes some work to implement a heuristic that will truly add value to your pipeline. Specifically, whether you are looking for a good heuristic or you are planning to develop your own heuristic, it needs to be able to tick a series of boxes.

First of all, the heuristic needs to be well-defined. Heuristics that are generic are probably going to yield more problems than they solve, as they will most likely require many parameters in order to be useful. If you have the option to choose a more specific heuristic with fewer parameters, it would be best to go with that option. There are exceptions to this, of course, such as some fundamentally innovative heuristics, like a new type of average or a new dispersion metric, but most people are not equipped or willing to create such high-level heuristics. Such an endeavor would require advanced inter-disciplinary know-how coupled with a highly original approach to building new heuristics.

Another important box to tick is scalability. A good heuristic has to be able to scale, which is equivalent to it being computationally inexpensive. Needless to say, heuristics that scale well are very applicable to data science, particularly when tackling big data.

In addition, a good heuristic is comprehensive, and to a great extent, intuitive. This does not mean that using a heuristic is easy, but it definitely doesn't require you to read a user manual in order to utilize it. Under the hood, a heuristic may be complex to the untrained eye, but it should not require a lot of effort to apply it to your problem or to test its functionality.

Moreover, a good heuristic tends to be versatile. This does not mean that it is going to be like a Swiss Army Knife, but it can still be applicable to a variety of different problems or datasets, sometimes in the same category (e.g. classification-related). No matter, if you are going to build a heuristic, you do not want it to apply only to one or two problems.

The final box to tick has to do with the heuristic being as assumption-free as possible. If it comes with a large number of assumptions, it is bound to have unnecessary complexities that are probably going to make it problematic in certain situations (probably ones that you cannot foresee at first). Also, an assumption-free style is more closely related to the data-driven approach, which constitutes the core philosophy of heuristics. The more assumptions a heuristic has, especially if they are about the distributions of the data it uses, the less usefulness it is going to have in general.

Some Final Considerations on Heuristics

Heuristics may not always be the way to go for a given problem. However, they may still yield some insight to the data at hand. After all, the data science pipeline is not a linear process, so trying out different things is not only allowed, but expected to some degree. Therefore, exploring the applicability of a few heuristics in your project is definitely worth trying, regardless of whether the corresponding code makes it to production. After all, many heuristics lend themselves to data exploration only, so not everything you use needs to be deployed on the cloud/cluster afterwards.

Also, sometimes the best way to learn something is to try it out like no one is watching. This is particularly applicable when it comes to heuristics. If this makes sense to you, and you find that it can be a way to express your creativity in a productive manner, go ahead and build a few heuristics of your own. Who knows? Maybe a couple of them will catch on and make things easier for everyone in the data science field. And if they don't make it to the community, you can still benefit from them and gain a better understanding of the lesser known aspects of information in the making.

Summary

A heuristic in data science is an empirical metric or process that aims to provide some useful tool or insight to facilitate a data science method or project. Heuristics can be viewed as information in the making, as they provide a variety of insights directly based on your data that facilitate the extraction of useful information from the data at hand. This information can be used as is or be incorporated into the models you build.

Problems that are complex or peculiar in a way, making conventional approaches to solving them impractical, usually lend themselves to heuristics. AI systems greatly depend on heuristics in order to function and yield a performance capable of adding value to a project. Particularly when it comes to avoiding over-fitting and finding an efficient way to train these systems, heuristics are a great asset.

Heuristics have a variety of applications in data science, such as:

- **Machine learning** – improving models through changing their internal workings, or through a more meaningful measurement of their performance (e.g. custom cost functions)
- **Data engineering** – facilitating the creation/transformation of features through heuristics in a creative way so that the resulting dataset is as information-rich as possible
- **Feature evaluation** – assessing the predictive potential of a feature or a set of features in relation to a target variable
- **Other** – such as ensembles

Some key characteristics of a good heuristic are:

- **Being well-defined** – abstract or overly generic heuristics are not helpful in practice
- **Being scalable** – heuristics need to be computationally cheap so that they can be applicable in scale
- **Being comprehensive and intuitive** – easy to understand heuristics are far more useful and applicable in practice
- **Being versatile** – heuristics are better off not being too specialized, and reusable in different problems, even if these problems are all of the same category
- **Having as few assumptions as possible** – fewer assumptions make the heuristic more widely applicable and free of excessive parameters

Heuristics are worth trying out in a data science project, even if you do not always make use of them in production. The best way to delve into heuristics is to try building your own for the data analytics problems you are tackling.

CHAPTER 12

The Role of AI in Data Science

Although Artificial Intelligence (AI) has been around for a few decades now, it is only since it has been utilized in data science that it has become mainstream. Before that, it was an esoteric technology that would be seen in relation to robotics or some highly sophisticated computer system, poised to destroy humanity. In reality, AI is mainly a set of fairly intelligent algorithms that are useful wherever they apply, as well as in the field of computer science that is involved in their development and application.

Even if there are a few success stories out there that help AI make the news and the marketing campaigns, more often than not, they are not the best resource in data science, since there are other resources that are better and more widely applicable (e.g. some dimensionality reduction methods and the feature engineering techniques). Plus, when they do make sense in a data science project, they require a lot of fine-tuning. AI is not a panacea, though it can be a useful tool to have in your toolbox, particularly if you find yourself working for a large company with access to lots of decent data.

In this chapter, we will take a look at various aspects of AI and how AI relates to data science including the problems AI solves, the different types of AI systems applied in data science, and considerations about AI's role in data science. This is not going to be an in-depth treatise on the AI techniques used in data science. Rather it will be more of an overview and a set of guidelines related to AI in data science. The information provided can serve as a good opportunity to develop a sense of perspective about AI and its relationship to data science.

Problems AI Solves

AI is an important group of technologies. It has managed to offer a holistic perspective in problem-solving since its inception. The idea is that with AI, a computer system will be able to frame the problem it needs to solve and solve it without having anyone hard-code it into a program. This is why AI programs have always been mostly practical, down-to-earth systems that intend, sometimes successfully, to emulate human reasoning (not just a predetermined set of rules). This is especially useful if you think about the problems engineers and scientists have faced in the past few decades, problems that are highly complex and practically impossible to solve analytically.

For example, the famous traveling salesman problem (TSP) has been a recurring problem that logistics organizations have been tackling for years. Even if its framing is quite straight-forward, an exact solution to it is hard to find (nearly impossible) for real life scenarios, where the number of locations the traveler plans to visit is non-trivial. Yet, given enough computing resources, it is possible to find an exact (analytical) solution to it, though most people opt for an AI-based one. AI is not the best route out there in this case, but it is close enough to make the solution valuable and also practical. What good would a solution be if it took the whole day to compute, using a bunch of computers, even if it were the most accurate solution out there? Would such an approach be scalable or cost-effective? In other words, would it be *intelligent*?

Most AI systems tackle more sophisticated problems, where the option of obtaining an ideal solution is not only impractical but also impossible. In fact, the majority of problems in applied science are nothing but approximations, and that's perfectly acceptable. Nowadays, it is usually mathematicians that opt for analytical solutions, and even among this group, some of them are willing to compromise for the purpose of practicality. Opting for an analytical solution may have its appeal, but there are many cases where it's just not worth it, especially if there are numeric methods that accomplish a good enough result in a fraction of the time.

AI is more than mathematics though, even if at its core it deals with optimization in one way or another. It is also about connecting the macro-level with the micro-level. This is why it is ideal for solving complex problems that often lack the definition required to tackle them efficiency. As the interface of AI becomes closer to what we are used to (e.g. everyday language), this is bound to become more obvious, the corresponding AI systems more mainstream. The amount of data that needs to be crunched in order for this idea to have a shot at becoming a possibility is mind-boggling. This is where data science comes in.

Data science problems that use AI are those that have highly non-linear search spaces or complex relationships among the variables involved. Also, problems where performance is of paramount importance tend to lend themselves to AI based approaches.

Types of AI Systems Used in Data Science

There are several types of AI systems utilized in data science. Most of them fall under one of two categories: deep learning networks and autoencoders. All of these AI systems are some form of an *artificial neural network (ANN)*, a robust system that is generally assumption-free. There are also AI systems that are not ANNs, and we will briefly take a look at them too.

An ANN is a graph that maps the flow of data as it undergoes certain, usually non-linear, transformations. The nodes of this graph are called *neurons,* and the function involving the transformation of the data as it goes through these neurons is called the *transference function.* The neurons are organized in layers, each of which can represent the inputs of the ANN (the features), a transformation of these features (or meta-features), or the outputs. In the case of predictive analytics ANNs, the outputs are related to the target variable. Also, the connections among the various neurons are called weights, and their exact values are figured out in the training phase of the system.

ANNs have been proven to be able to approximate any function, though more complex functions require more neurons and usually more layers too. The most widely used ANNs are also the predecessors of deep learning networks, the feed forward kind.

Deep Learning Networks

This is the most popular AI system used in data science, as it covers a series of ANNs designed to tackle a variety of problems. What all of these ANNs have in common is that there are a large number of layers in them, allowing them to build a series of higher-level features and the system to go deeper into the data it is analyzing. This kind of architecture is not new, but only recently has the computing infrastructure been able to catch up with the computational cost that these systems accrue. Also, the advent of parallel computing and the low cost of GPUs enabled this AI technology to become more widespread and accessible to data scientists everywhere. The use of this technology in data science is referred to as deep learning (DL).

Deep learning networks come in all sorts, ranging from the basic ones that aim to perform conventional classification and regression tasks to more specialized ones that are designed for specific tasks that are not possible with conventional ANNs. For example, recurrent neural networks (RNNs) are a useful kind of DL network, focusing on capturing the signal in time-series data. This is done by having connections that go both forward and backward in the network, generating loops in the flow of data through the system. This architecture allows RNNs to be particularly useful for word prediction and other NLP related applications (e.g. language translation), image processing, and finding appropriate captions for pictures or video clips. However, this does not mean that RNNs cannot be used in other areas not particularly related to dynamic data.

When it comes to analyzing highly complex data consisting of a large number of features, many of which are somewhat correlated, convolutional neural networks (CNNs) are one of the best tools to use. The idea is to combine multi-level analysis with resampling in the same system, thereby optimizing the system's performance without depending on the sophisticated data engineering that would be essential for this kind of data. If this sounds convoluted, you can think of a CNN as an AI system that is fed a multi-dimensional array of data at a time, rather than a single matrix, as is usually the case with other ANNs. This allows it to build a series of feature sets based on its inputs, gradually growing in terms of abstraction.

So, for the case of an image (having three distinct channels, one for each primary color), the CNN layers include features corresponding to crude characteristics of the image, such as the dominance of a particular color on one side of the image, or the presence of some linear pattern. All of these features may look very similar to the human eye. Once these features are analyzed further, we start to differentiate a bit. These more sophisticated features (present in the next layer) correspond to subtler patterns, such as the presence of two or more colors in the image, each having a particular shape. In the layer that follows, the features will have an even higher level of differentiation, capturing specific shapes and line/color patterns that may resonate with our understanding of the image. These layers are called convolution layers. In the CNN, there are also specialized sets of features that are called pooling layers. The role of these layers is to reduce the size of the feature representation in the other layers, making the process of abstraction more manageable and efficient. The most common kind of pooling involves taking the maximum value of a set of neurons from the previous layer; this is called max pooling. CNNs are ideal for image and video processing, as well as NLP applications.

Autoencoders

These are a particular kind of ANN that, although akin to DL networks, are focused on dimensionality reduction through a better feature representation. As we saw in the previous section, the inner layers of a DL network correspond to features it creates using the original features. Also known as meta-features, these can be used either for finding a good enough mapping to the targets, or to original features again. The latter is what autoencoders do, with the inner-most layer being the actual result of the process once the system is fully trained.

So why is all of this a big deal? After all, you can perform dimensionality reduction with other methods and not have to worry about fine-tuning parameters to do so. Statistical methods, which have traditionally been the norm for this task, are highly impractical and loaded with assumptions. For example, the covariance matrix, which is used as the basis of PCA, one of the most popular dimensionality reduction methods, is comprised of all the pairwise covariances of the features in the original set. These covariances are not by any means a reliable metric for establishing the strength of the similarity of the features. For these to work well, the features need a great deal of engineering beforehand, and even then, the PCA method may not yield the best reduced feature set possible. Also, methods like PCA (including ICA and SVD methods) take a lot of time when it comes to large datasets, making them highly impractical for many data science projects. Autoencoders bypass all these issues, though you may still need to pass the number of meta-features as a parameter, corresponding to the number of neurons in the inner-most layer.

Other Types of AI Systems

Apart from these powerful AI systems for data science, there are also some other ones that are less popular. Also, note that although there are many other ANN-based systems (see http://bit.ly/2dKrPbQ for a comprehensive overview of them), AI methods for data science include other architectures as well.

For example, fuzzy logic systems have been around since the 1970's and were among the first AI frameworks. Also, they are versatile enough to be useful to applications beyond data science. Even if they are not used much today (mainly because they are not easy to calibrate), they are a viable alternative for certain problems when interpretability is of paramount importance, while there is also reliable information from experts that can be coded into fuzzy logic rules.

Another kind of AI system that is useful, though not as data science specific, is optimization systems, or optimizers. These are algorithms that aim to find the best value of a function (i.e. its maximum or minimum) given a set of conditions. Optimizers are essential as parts of other systems, including most machine learning systems. However, optimizers are applicable in data engineering processes too, such as feature selection. As we saw in the previous chapters, optimizers rely heavily on heuristics in order to function.

Extreme Learning Machines (ELM's) are another AI system designed for data science. They may share a similar architecture with ANNs, but their training is completely different. They optimize the weights of only the last layer's connections with the outputs. This unique approach to data learning makes them extremely fast and simple to work with. Also, given enough hidden layers,

ELMs perform exceptionally in terms of accuracy, making them a viable alternative to other high-end data science systems. Unfortunately, ELMs are not as popular as they could be, since not that many people know about them.

AI Systems Using Data Science

Beyond these AI systems, there are other ones too that do not contribute to data science directly, but make use of it instead. These are more like applications of AI, which are equally important to the systems that facilitate data science processes. As these applications gain more ground, it could be that your work as a data scientist is geared toward them, with data science being a tool in their pipeline. This depicts its variety of applications and general usefulness in the AI domain.

Computer Vision

Computer vision is the field of computer science that involves the perception of visual stimuli by computer systems, especially robots. This is done by analyzing the data from visual sensors using AI systems, performing some pattern recognition on them and passing that information to a computer in order to facilitate other tasks (e.g. movement in the case of a robot). One of the greatest challenges of computer vision is being able to do all that in real time. Analyzing an image is not hard if you are familiar with image processing methods, but performing such an analysis in a fraction of a second is a different story. This is why practical computer vision had been infeasible before AI took off in data science.

Although computer vision focuses primarily on robotics, it has many other applications. For example, it can be used in CCTV systems, drones, and most interestingly, self-driving cars. Also, it would not be far-fetched to one day see such systems making an appearance in phone cameras. This way, augmented reality add-ons can evolve to something beyond just a novelty, and be able to offer very practical benefits, thanks to computer vision. Since the development of RNNs and other AI systems, computer vision has become highly practical and is bound to continue being a powerful application of AI for many years to come.

Chatbots

Chatbots are all the rage when it comes to AI applications, especially among those who use them as personal assistants (e.g. Amazon Echo). Even though a voice operated system may seem different than a conventional chatbot, which only understands text, they are in essence the same technology under the hood. A chatbot is any AI system that can communicate with its user using natural language (usually English) and carry out basic tasks. Chatbots are particularly useful in information retrieval and administrative tasks. However, they can also do more complex things, such as place an order for you (e.g. in the case of Alexa, the Amazon virtual assistant chatbot). Also, chatbots are able to ask their own questions, whenever they find that the user's input is noisy or easy to misinterpret.

Chatbots are made possible by a number of systems. First of all, they have an NLP system in place that analyzes the user's text. This way it is able to understand key objects. In this pipeline, there is also what is called an intent identifier, which aims to figure out what the intention of the user is when interacting with the chatbot. Based on the results of this, the chatbot can then carry out the task that seems more relevant, or provide a response about its inability to carry out the task. If it is programmed accordingly, it can even make small talk, though its responses are limited. After the chatbot carries out the task, it provides the user with a confirmation and usually prompts for additional inputs by the user. Some random delays can happen in the conversation in order to make it appear more realistic, as the chatbot learns to pick up new words (if it is sophisticated enough).

The fact that a chatbot's whole operation is feasible in real time is something remarkable and made possible by incorporating data science into how it analyzes the inputs it receives. Synthesizing an answer based on the results it wants to convey is fairly easy (often relying on a template), but figuring out the intent and the objects involved may not be so straight-forward, considering how many different users may interact with the chatbot. Also, in the case of a voice-operated chatbot, an additional layer exists in the pipeline, involving the analysis of the user's voice and the transcription of text corresponding to it.

Artificial Creativity

Artificial creativity is an umbrella of various applications of AI that have to do with the creation of works of art or the solution of highly complex problems, such as the design of car parts and the better use of resources in a data center. Artificial creativity is not something new, though it has only recently managed to achieve such levels that it is virtually indistinguishable from human creativity. In some cases (e.g. the tackling of complex problems), it performs even better than the creativity of domain experts (humans). An example of artificial creativity in the domain of painting is the idea of using a DL network trained with various images from the works of a famous artist, and then using another image in conjunction with this network so that parts of the image are changed to make it similar to the images of the network it is trained on. This creates a new image that is similar to both, but emulates the artistic style of the training set with excellence, as if the new image was created using the same technique.

RNNs are great for artificial creativity, especially when the domain is text. Although the result in this case may not be as easy to appreciate as in most cases, it is definitely interesting. At the very least, it can help people better comprehend the system's functionality, as it is often perceived as a black box (just like any other ANN-based system).

Other AI Systems Using Data Science

Beyond these applications of AI that make use of data science, there are several more, too many to mention in this chapter. I will focus on the ones that stand out, mainly due to the impact they have on our lives.

First of all, we have navigation systems. These we may have come to take for granted, but they are in reality AI systems based on geolocation data and a set of heuristics. Some people think of them as simple optimizers of a path in a graph, but these days they are more sophisticated than that. Many navigation systems take into account other factors, such as traffic, road blockages, and even user preferences (such as avoiding certain roads). The optimization may be on the total time or the distance, while they often provide an estimate of the fuel consumption in the case of a motor vehicle the user predefines. Also, doing all the essential calculations in real-time is a challenge of its own, which these systems tackle gracefully. What's more, many of them can operate offline, which is still more impressive, as the resources available on a mobile device are significantly limited compared to those on the cloud.

Another AI application related to navigation systems is voice synthesizers; the latter are a common component of the former. Yet voice synthesizers have grown beyond the requirements of a navigation system. They are used in other frameworks as well, such as ebook readers. To synthesize voice accurately and without a robotic feel to it is a challenge that has been made possible through sophisticated analysis of audio data and the reproduction of it using DL networks.

Automatic translation systems are another kind of AI application based on data science, particularly NLP. However, it is not as simple as looking up words in a dictionary and replacing them. No matter how many rules are used in this approach, the result is bound to be mechanical, not "feeling right" to the end user.

However, modern translation systems make use of sophisticated methods that look at the sentence as a whole before attempting to translate it. Also, they try to understand what is going on and take into account translations of similar text by human translators. As a result, the translated text is not only accurate, but more comprehensive, even if it is not always as good as that of a professional translator.

Some Final Considerations on AI

AI systems have great potential, especially when used in tandem with data science processes. However, they, just like data science in its first years, are over-ridden by a lot of hype, making it difficult to discern fact from fiction. It is easy to succumb to the excessive optimism about these technologies and adopt the idea that AI is a panacea that will solve all of our problems, data science related or otherwise. Some people have even built a faith system around Artificial Intelligence. As data scientists, we need to see things for what they are instead of getting lost in other people's interpretations. AI is a great field, and its systems are very useful. However, they are just algorithms and computer systems built on these algorithms. They may be linked to various devices and make their abilities easy to sense, but this does not change the fact that they are just another technology.

Maybe one day, if everything evolves smoothly and we take enough careful steps towards that direction, we can have something that more closely resembles human thinking and reasoning in AI. Let us not confuse this possibility with the certainty of what we observe. The latter we can measure and reason with, while the former we can only speculate about. So, let's make the most that we can with AI systems, whenever they apply, without getting carried away. Taking the human factor out of the equation may not only be difficult, but also dangerous, especially when it comes to liability matters. More on that in the chapter that follows.

Summary

AI is a field of computer science dealing with the emulation of human intelligence using computer systems and its applications in a variety of domains, as well as in data science. AI is important, particularly in data science, as it allows for the tackling of more complex problems, some of which cannot be solved through conventional approaches.

The problems that are most relevant to AI technologies are those that have one or more of the following characteristics: highly non-linear search spaces, complex relationships among their variables, and performance being a key factor.

Artificial Neural Networks (ANNs) are a key system category for many AI systems used in data science.

There are several types of AI systems focusing on data science, grouped into the following categories:

- **Deep learning networks** – These are sophisticated ANNs, having multiple layers, and being able to provide a more robust performance for a variety of tasks. This category of AI systems includes Recurrent Neural Networks (RNNs) and Convolutional Neural Networks (CNNs), among others.
- **Autoencoders** – Similar to DL networks, this AI system is ideal for dimensionality reduction and able to handle large datasets too
- **Other** – This includes Fuzzy Logic based systems, optimizers, Extreme Learning Machines, and more

There are various AI systems employing data science on the back-end, such as:

- **Computer vision** – This kind of AI system involves the perception of visual data by computer systems, especially robots
- **Chatbots** – These are useful AI systems that interact with humans in natural language
- **Artificial creativity** – This is not so much an AI system, but an application of AI related to the use of sophisticated AI systems for the creation of artistic works or for solving highly complex problems
- **Other** – There are also other AI systems employing data science, such as navigation systems, voice synthesizers, automatic translation systems

AI systems are a great resource, but they are not a panacea. It is good to be mindful about their usefulness without getting too overzealous about AI and its potential.

CHAPTER 13

Data Science Ethics

We saw in the previous chapter that AI can facilitate the data science process by a great deal of automating. However, even if some parts of the pipeline become automated, certain aspects of data science will remain untouched. They cannot be fully automated due to their non-mechanical nature. Ethics is one part of the process that is currently beyond automation.

In this chapter, we will examine various aspects of data science ethics, such as why it is important, the role of confidentiality (mainly privacy, data anonymization, and data security), as well as licensing matters. Using ethics in our practices elevate the role of the data scientist and enables us to offer something more than interesting insights and pretty products.

The Importance of Ethics in Data Science

Ethics is not something that is just nice to have, as some people think, especially those in the technical professions. In fact, it can be more significant than the actual analytics work that we are requested to undertake, especially when it comes to matters of privacy, security, and other potential liabilities that often outweigh the potential benefit from harvesting the data at hand. One of the key aspects of ethics is that it enables constructive and mutually beneficial relationships to come about in every organization. In addition, data science can become dangerous without some ethical foundation behind it. What's worse, in some cases it does. This is especially true when there is sensitive data involved, such as financial, medical, or other kinds of personal data. Ethics is like a fail-safe, keeping data science in check when it comes to these kinds of situations.

These days, anyone can take a course in data science, read a book or two, watch a few videos, play around with a few datasets, and get the basics down of the data science craft. Although this is great, it does not make someone a data science professional. However, with ethics, all this skill can be put to good use, making the difference between a professional data scientist and one who just possesses the relevant know-how.

Confidentiality Matters

Confidentiality means keeping information accessible only to the people that really need to know it. Although this is often associated with encryption, a process for turning comprehensible information into gibberish in order to keep the information inaccessible, confidentiality involves more than just that. In the world of digital information, confidentiality is a very valuable asset, which unfortunately does not get the attention it needs in the context of data science. As data scientists, we need to take an ethical approach to confidentiality much the same as a doctor or a lawyer, especially when dealing with sensitive data. Doing otherwise is without a doubt unethical.

The parts of confidentiality that are most relevant to the data science field are *privacy, data anonymization,* and *data security.* In this section, we will look at each one of these concepts as they correspond to data science, and learn about how we can take them into account so that our work remains ethical.

Privacy

Protecting data from outsiders involves many different processes. One of the most important is privacy. Privacy is key in data science, especially in projects where sensitive data is involved, since it can easily "break" an organization. Even companies that have a good reputation and have gained their clients' trust can lose everything if there is a privacy issue in their data. Take for example the case of Yahoo. Management blunders aside, Yahoo's data privacy was severely compromised, which led to the loss of trust and respect from clients and society at large. Data exposed included names, email addresses, phone numbers, hashed passwords, and more, for over 500 million user accounts.

Ensuring privacy in the data handled in a data science project should always be kept in mind. If the data is being processed inside a company, this should not be an issue, as there are usually specialized professionals ensuring that everything inside the office space is private and secure. In the cases when you wish to work from home or have to be on the road for a business trip, the best and most secure option would be to use a virtual private network (VPN) or a TCP tunneling technique for connecting to the servers where the data is.

This is due to the fact that all sensitive data tends to be stored in private servers. When outside of the private servers, its privacy of the data therein could be compromised. The worst part of all this is that if this happens, you will probably not be aware of it when it happens. Unlike movies, hackers in the real-world do not leave witty messages on the computers they gain access to, even though some of the more amateur ones may accidentally leave some kind of trail. Whatever the case, it would be best to make it as hard as possible for them to access your data. If it takes too much effort to compromise your data's privacy, they will probably move on to their next target.

One thing to keep in mind as far as privacy is concerned is that you ought to think of the worst-case-scenario in advance. This can be a great motivator and guide for the lengths you will need to go to in order to ensure that all data you use remains private throughout the duration of your project. Also, this can help you anticipate the vulnerabilities of your process and ensure that no private data is compromised.

Finally, it is important to remember that it is not just data that needs to be kept private, but metadata (data about the data) too. Also, someone's privacy can be compromised not only with a single piece of data (e.g. their social security number), but also with a combination of things, such as a medical condition, a location, and their demographical makeup.

Data Anonymization

Good confidentiality also means making sure your data is anonymous. In other words, all personal identified information (aka PII) needs to be removed or hidden so that it is not possible for anyone to find the people behind the data points analyzed. Data anonymization not only helps mitigate the risk of the data being abused by third parties, but also removes any temptation you may have to abuse it yourself.

Data anonymization makes data useless to people who would gain access to it, when it comes to exploiting the people behind it. This way, the data is useful only for your data analytics projects, through the patterns it has as a whole. Each data point on its own is practically useless. This kind of confidentiality is essential in the finance industry, where payment data is common. However, even if you are working for a company that deals in online transactions and your projects involve credit card data, you have to pay attention to data anonymization.

If you have to use the variables containing sensitive information in your models, you can try mapping a hashing value to them. This way, the uniqueness of their values will be maintained, and the actual hashes will be meaningless to everyone accessing them. You can think of hashing as a transformation that is easy to do in one direction but extremely time-consuming, if not impossible, to reverse. Reversing a hash is equivalent to breaking an encryption code.

Since you do not want to take any risks when anonymizing these variables, it is a good practice to apply some "salt" in the hashing process, to ensure that it is even harder to break. The salt is usually a few random characters added to every data point, and it ensures a much stronger level of anonymization.

Similar to the privacy aspect of confidentiality, when dealing with data anonymization, you ought to consider the worst thing that could happen if the data you anonymize is leaked. This way you will have an accurate estimate of how much time you should dedicate to the whole process and ensure that you take the right steps to keep all sensitive data anonymous.

Data Security

Data security is another part of confidentiality, and it is probably the one most widely used, even outside the data science field. If you have bought something on an online store, or have accessed your bank account through the web or an app, you have used a form of data security, even if you were unaware of it. Without data security, all online transfers of information would be extremely risky and inviable.

The main methods that are used when it comes to native security are *encryption* and *steganography*. The first has to do with turning the data into gibberish, as we mentioned previously, while the latter is all about hiding it in plain sight by inserting it into some usually large data file, such as an image, an audio clip, or even a video. You can use both of these methods in conjunction for extra security (i.e. encrypt the data and then apply steganography to it).

When it comes to security beyond your computer's hard drive, you have to take additional precautions. This is because in most cases your computer can be accessed through the Internet if certain ports are left open. Keeping ports open can be useful at times (e.g. for software updates), but it is a common liability that is favorable by black-hat hackers. So, keeping vital ports in your computer closed when you don't use them is a good way to keep hackers at bay. Usually a good firewall program can help you manage that easily.

Naturally, it is also important to have secure software on your computer and especially a secure operating system (OS). This is particularly important for whatever programs you have set up to run on the cloud (e.g. APIs). Although certain OSes are more secure than others, how secure your computer is depends on how well you secure it, regardless of the OS you have. Even the most secure OS is vulnerable to hackers if it is not set up properly. For this kind of security, it would be best to consult a network engineer or a white-hat hacker.

Finally, storing important data is something that every data scientist has to deal with on his day-to-day work, so it is important that it is done properly. Whether it is passwords, data, or code, everything needs to be stored in a secure location, preferably in an encrypted format. Remember that any programming code you produce is part of your organization's intellectual property, so it should be treated as an asset. The passwords are best kept in a password database, such as KeePass (KeePassX for Linux systems) or LastPass. Also, all important files are better off backed up in a remote location. Backing things up is something that needs to take place on a regular basis, which is why many back-up programs offer an automation mechanism for this.

If you apply these security pointers, your data is bound to remain safe. In case this seems like overkill, remember that it only takes one security breach to jeopardize a company's assets and potentially its reputation. Security matters are not only part of data science ethics, but also of your organization's integrity.

Licensing Matters

Let us now examine licensing a bit, a topic that usually doesn't get any attention in data science. Even though we often do not pay much attention to copyright when using programs and content we encounter on the web when it comes to personal use, infringement of copyright is a serious issue, especially when the copyrighted material is used commercially. Therefore, the ethical approach to this matter is to pay close attention whenever handling any material with the © symbol.

Keep in mind that even data can be under copyright if it is proprietary, so using it for a data science project may require a certain kind of licensing. This is why you must be extra careful when scraping data from the web. The data in that case may be there for viewing, but not for using it for other purposes.

When it comes to open-source software, there is no issue with copyright, as it is usually free to use (oftentimes there is a different licensing in place, such as Creative Commons (CC), also known as copyleft). Sometimes, this software may not be free for commercial purposes, so keep that in mind. Also, just because something is free now does not mean that it is going to be free in the future.

In addition, if you make an innovation, it is a good idea to check for existing patents to minimize the risk of getting sued by some other inventor. This is particularly important if you plan to use that innovation commercially, which is what patents are for.

Finally, if you make use of images in your projects (e.g. as part of a presentation or a GUI for a data product) make sure that they are under CC license. If no licensing information is available for a given image, always assume that you will need to get permission before using it. Even if the owner of the graphic has no issue with you using it, the ethical way to approach it is to ask for permission and document their response.

Other Ethical Matters

Beyond these basic aspects of data science ethics, there are other things that are also important. These are not specific to data science, as they have to do with professional ethics in general. For example, being able to meet deadlines is an important ethical matter, especially when dealing with time-sensitive projects, as is often the case in data science. Also, making sure that everything is documented and passed on to other members of the team is essential in order to perform data science properly. Maintaining an objective stance regarding experiments is another issue of ethics that is paramount when it comes to testing hypotheses. After all, the excessive pressure of publishing papers that characterizes academia is non-existent in data science.

Some Final Considerations on Ethics

Ethics is often confused with morality, and although related, they are not the same. For starters, morality is internal and relates to a set of principles or values as well as a sense of right and wrong, while ethics is external and has to do with a set of behaviors and attitudes. Also, even if morality may take many years to develop, ethics is always within reach. This is because ethics is external, which even though it often stems from morality, it can exist independently.

Beyond the duality of ethics and morality, there are several other things related to ethics that are worth mentioning. For example, ethics is a matter of personal priorities. As such, it may not be asked of you directly or checked afterward. However, it is still expected of you, especially if you are in a responsible position in an organization, or you are branding yourself as a stand-alone data science consultant.

Summary

Ethics is a part of the data science profession that cannot be automated and which adds a lot of value to process, even if it is not usually perceived immediately. Ethics in data science involves the following:

- **Confidentiality** – making sure the data is accessed only by the people who are supposed to access it. It involves privacy, data anonymization, and data security.
- **Licensing** – handling copyright matters and ensuring that no one is sued by using external material and data in your projects
- **Privacy** is an essential part of confidentiality related to keeping data accessible only to those who need to access it. This involves not just data but also metadata and anything that can reveal a person's identity through a piece of data or a combination of things.
- **Data anonymization** is about changing data to ensure that confidentiality is maintained
- **Data security** is a common process that involves keeping data safe from external hazards, such as hackers and unpredictable catastrophes

Ethics is different from morality, although they are interlinked. Morality is an internal matter related to one's values, while ethics is an external matter, related to one's attitude and the manifestation of certain moral principles.

Ethics is one of the key differentiators between a professional and an amateur, especially in the data science field.

CHAPTER 14

Future Trends and How to Remain Relevant

Data science is a dynamic field; it is constantly changing. Therefore, keeping up with new developments is not just advisable, it is also expected (and necessary in staying relevant to employers and clients for that matter). Otherwise, your know-how is bound to become obsolete sooner or later, making you a less marketable professional. In order to avoid this, it is important to learn about the newest trends and have strategies in place about remaining relevant in this ever-changing field.

In this chapter, we will examine general trends in data science that are bound to affect it in the coming decade. This includes the role of AI, the future of big data, new programming paradigms, and the rise of Hadoop alternatives. In addition, we will look at ways to remain relevant in data science, such as the versatilist approach, data science research, continuously educating yourself, collaborative projects, and mentoring. This chapter may not guarantee that you will become future-proof, but it will help you to be more prepared so that you ride the waves of change instead of being swallowed by them.

General Trends in Data Science

Even though data science is a chaotic system and the many changes it experiences over time are next to impossible to predict, there are some general patterns, or trends, that appear to emerge. By learning about the trends of our field, you will be more equipped to prepare yourself and adapt effectively as data science evolves.

The Role of AI in the Years to Come

Apart from the hype about AI, the fact is that AI has made an entrance in data science, and it is here to stay. This does not mean that everything in the future will be AI-based, but it is likely that AI methods, like deep learning networks, will become more and more popular. It is possible that some conventional methods will still be around due to their simplicity or interpretability (e.g. decision trees), but they will probably not be the go-to methods in production.

Keep in mind that AI is an evolving field as well, so the methods that are popular today in data science may not necessarily be popular in the future. New ANN types and configurations are constantly being developed, while ANN ensembles have been shown to be effective as well. Always keep an open mind about AI and the different ways it applies to data science. If you have the researcher mindset and have the patience for it, it may be worth it to do a post-grad program in AI.

Big Data: Getting Bigger and More Quantitative

It may come as a surprise to many people that big data is getting more quantitative since the majority of it is comprised of text and other kinds of unstructured data, that's not harnessed yet, often referred to as *dark data*. However, as the *Internet of Things* (IoT) becomes more widespread, sensor data becomes increasingly available. Although much of it is not directly usable, it is quantitative, and as such, capable of being processed extensively with various techniques (such as statistics).

In addition, most of the AI systems out there work with mainly quantitative data (even discrete data needs to be converted to a series of binary variables in order to be used). Therefore, lots of data acquisition processes tend to focus on this kind of data to populate the databases they are linked to, making this kind of data more abundant.

As for the growth of big data, this is not a surprise, considering that the various processes that generate data, whether from the environment (through sensors) or via our online activities (through web services), grow exponentially. Also, storage is becoming cheaper and cheaper, so collecting this data is more cost-effective than ever before. The fact that there are many systems in place that can analyze that data make it a valuable resource worth collecting.

New Programming Paradigms

Although Object-Oriented Programming (OOP) is the dominant programming paradigm at the moment, this is bound to change in the years to come. Already some robust functional languages have made their appearance in the field (see Chapter 4 for a recap), and it is likely that languages of that paradigm are not going away any time soon. It is possible that other programming paradigms will arise as well. It would not be far-fetched to see graphical programming having a more pronounced appearance in data science, much like the one featured in the Azure ML ecosystem.

Regardless, OOP will not be going away completely, but those too attached to it may have a hard time adapting to what is to come. This is why I strongly recommend looking into alternative languages to the OOP ones, as well as bridge packages (i.e. packages linking scripts of one language to another).

In addition, if you are good at the logic behind programming and have the patience to go through its documentation, any changes in the programming aspect of data science shouldn't be a problem. After all, most new languages are made to be closer to the user and are accompanied by communities of users, making them more accessible than ever before. As long as you take the time to practice them and go through code on particular problems, the new programming paradigms should be an interesting endeavor rather than something intimidating or tedious.

The Rise of Hadoop Alternatives

Even though Hadoop has been around for some time, there are other alternatives in the big data arena. Lately, these big data governance platforms have been gaining ground, leaving Hadoop behind both in terms of speed and ease of use. Ecosystems like Microsoft's Azure ML, IBM's Infosphere, and Amazon's cloud services, have made a dent in Hadoop's dominance, and this trend doesn't show signs of slowing down.

What's more, there are several other systems nowadays that are on the software layer above Hadoop and which handle all the tasks that the Hadoop programs would. In other words, Hadoop's role has diminished to merely offering its file system (HDFS), while all the querying, scheduling, and processing of the data is handled by alternative systems like Spark, Storm, H2O, and Kafka. Despite its evolution, Hadoop is getting left behind as an all-in-one solution, even if it may still remain relevant in the years to come as a storage platform.

Other Trends

Beyond the aforementioned trends, there are several other ones that may be useful for you to know. For example, there are several pieces of hardware that are becoming very relevant to data science, as they largely facilitate computationally heavy processes, such as training DL networks. GPUs, Tensor Processing Units (also known as TPUs, http://bit.ly/2rqk2bU), and other hardware are moving to the forefront of data science technology, changing the landscape of the computer systems where production level data science systems are deployed.

Also, with parallelization becoming more accessible to non-specialists, it is useful to remember that building private computer clusters may be easier than people think, as it is cost-effective to buy a bunch of mini-computers or even tiny-computers (e.g. Arduinos) and connect them in a cluster array. Of course, with cloud computing becoming more affordable and with it being easier to scale, it could be that the clusters on the cloud trend may continue as well.

There are also new deep learning systems, such as Amazon's MXnet, making certain AI systems more accessible to non-experts. A trend like this is bound to become the norm, since automation is already fairly commonplace in a variety of data science processes. As we saw earlier, AI is here to stay, so new deep learning systems may be very popular in the future, especially ones that incorporate a variety of programming frameworks.

Remaining Relevant in the Field

Remaining relevant in data science is fairly easy once you get into the right mindset and allow your curiosity and creativity to take charge. After all, we are not in the field just because it is a great place to be, but also because we are interested in the science behind it (hopefully!) and care about how it evolves. Understanding the trends of data science today may help in that as it can enhance our perspective and urge us to take action along these trends.

The Versatilist Data Scientist

There are some people who specialize in one thing, also known as specialists, and there are others who know a bit of everything, though they do not have a particularly noteworthy strength, also known as generalists. Both of these groups have their role to play in the market, and there is no good or bad between the two. However, there is a group that is better than either one of them, as it combines aspects of both: the *versatilists*.

A versatilist is a (usually technical) professional who is good at various things and particularly adept at one of them. This enables him to undertake a variety of roles, even if he only excels in one of them. Therefore, if someone else in his team has trouble with his tasks or is absent for some reason, the versatilist can undertake those tasks and deal with whatever problem comes about. Also, such a person is great at communicating with others, as there is a lot of common ground between him and his colleagues. This person can be a good leader too, once he gains enough experience in his craft.

Being a versatilist in data science is not easy, as the technologies involved are in constant flux. Yet, being a versatilist it is a guarantee for remaining relevant. Otherwise, you are subject to the demands of the market and other people's limited understanding of the field when it comes to recruiting. Also, being a versatilist in data science allows you to have a better understanding of the bigger picture and liaise with all sorts of professionals, within and outside the data science spectrum.

Data Science Research

If you are so inclined (especially if you already have a PhD), you may want to apply your research skills to data science. It might be easier than you think, considering that in most parts of data science, the methods used are fairly simple (especially the statistical models). Still, in the one area where some truly sophisticated models exist (AI), there is plenty of room for innovation. If you feel that your creativity is on par with your technical expertise, you may want to explore new methods of data modeling and perhaps data engineering too. At the very least, you will become more intimately familiar with the algorithms of data analytics and the essence of data science, namely the signal and the noise in the data.

If you find that your research is worthwhile, even if it is not groundbreaking, you can share it with the rest of the community as a package (Julia is always in need for such packages and it is an easy language to prototype in). Alternatively, you can write a white paper on it (to share with a selected few) and explore ways to commercialize it. Who knows? Maybe you can get a start-up going based on your work. At the very least, you will get more exposure to the dynamics of the field itself and gain a better understanding of the trends and how the field evolves.

The Need to Educate Oneself Continuously

No matter how extensive and thorough your education in data science is, there is always a need to continue to educate yourself if you want to remain relevant. This is easier than people think, since once you have the basics down and have assimilated the core concepts through practice and correcting mistakes. Perhaps a MOOC would be sufficient for some people, while scientific articles would be sufficient for others. In any case, you must not remain complacent, since the field is unforgiving to those who think they have mastered it.

Education in the field can come in various forms that go beyond the more formal channels (MOOCs and other courses). Although being focused on a specific medium for learning can be beneficial, it is often more practical to combine several mediums. For example, you might read articles about a new machine learning method, watch a video on a methodology or technique (preferably one of my videos on Safari Books!), read a good book on the subject, and participate in a data science competition.

Collaborative Projects

Collaborative projects are essential when it comes to remaining relevant in data science. This is not just because they can help you expand your expertise and perspective, something invaluable toward the beginning of your career, but they can also help you challenge yourself and discover new approaches to solving data science problems. When you are on your own, you may come up with some good ideas, but with no one to challenge them or offer alternatives, there is a danger of becoming somewhat complacent or self-assured, two challenging obstacles in any data scientist's professional development.

Collaborative projects may be commonplace when working for an organization, but sometimes it is necessary to go beyond that. That's what data science competitions and offshore projects are about. Although many of these competitions offer a skewed view of data science (as the data they have is often heavily processed), the challenges and benefits of working with other people remain. This is accentuated when there is no manager in place and all sense of order has to come from the team itself.

These kinds of working endeavors are particularly useful when the team is not close physically. Co-working is becoming more and more an online process rather than an in-person one, with collaborative systems like Slack and Github becoming more commonplace than ever. After all, most data science roles do not require someone to be in a particular location all the time in order to accomplish their tasks. Doing data science remotely is not always an easy task, but if the appropriate systems are in place (e.g. VPNs and a cloud infrastructure), it is not only possible, but preferable.

Collaborative projects can also expose you to data that you may not encounter in your everyday work. This data may require a special approach that you are not aware of (possibly something new). If you are serious about your role in these projects, you are bound to learn through this process, as you will be forced to go beyond your comfort zone and expand your know-how.

Mentoring

Mentoring is when someone knowledgeable and adept in a field shares his experience and advice with other people who are newer to the field. Although mentoring can be a formal endeavor, it can also be circumstantial, depending on the commitment of the people involved. Also, even though it is not compulsory, mentoring is strongly recommended, especially among new people in the field.

Unlike other more formal educational processes, mentoring is based on a one-on-one professional relationship, usually without any money involved between the mentor and the mentee (protégé). For the former, it is a way of giving back to the data science community, while for the latter, it is a way to learn from more established data scientists. Although mentoring is not a substitute for a data science course, it can offer you substantial information about matters that are not always covered in a course, such as ways to tackle problems that arise and strategic advice for your data science career.

Mentoring requires a great deal of commitment. This is not just to the professional relationship itself, but also to the data science field. It is easy to lose interest or become disheartened, especially if you are new to it, and even more so if you are struggling. Although a mentor can help you in that, he is not going to fight your battles for you. Much like mentors in other professions, a data science mentor is like a guide rather than a tutor.

Even if it is for a short period of time, mentoring is definitely helpful, especially if you are interested in going deeper into the inner workings of data science. Also, it can be of benefit to you regardless of your level, not just to newcomers. What's more, even if you are on the giving end of the mentoring relationship, you still have a lot to learn, especially on continuously improving your communication skills. If you have the chance to incorporate a mentoring dynamic in your data science life, it is definitely worth your time and can help you remain relevant (especially if you are a mentor).

Summary

Being aware of the trends of data science and having strategies in place about remaining relevant in the field enables you to remain an asset and make the most of your data science career.

Future trends in data science include:

- The role of AI becoming more paramount in data science, perhaps even the predominant paradigm
- Big Data getting bigger and more quantitative due to new technologies such as Internet of Things (IoT)
- New programming paradigms, such as functional programming, becoming more commonplace
- Hadoop alternatives, such as Spark, becoming the norm for handling Big Data
- Other trends, such as GPUs, TPUs, and other hardware, coming to the forefront of data science technology, as well as new DL systems, such as MXnet

AI is bound to evolve in the years to come, so it is advisable to remain up-to-date about it and perhaps even investigate ways of your own to develop it via a post-grad program.

Some of the ways to remain relevant in data science are:

- Cultivating the versatilist mindset, enabling you to undertake all sorts of data science roles across the pipeline
- Being aware of the limitations of existing data science methods and advancing them through research
- Developing a habit of educating yourself throughout your career, through a variety of educational mediums
- Participating in collaborative projects
- Mentoring, whether you are the mentor or the mentee

Final Words

In this book, I made an effort to help you enhance your perception and understanding of data science. It is my hope that you can use this knowledge to improve your data science work or to identify areas of the field where you would like to focus. At the very least, I hope you enjoyed it and had an opportunity to think about data science in an open-ended way, much like the pioneers of the field did, as well as many others currently making their way in the world of data science.

These days, many people want to reduce data science to a set of processes that can be automated or at least semi-automated through a series of high-level tools. Although this can sound attractive as an idea, it may be the case that such a task would be an oversimplification of data science and perhaps even a dangerous feat, as the mindset that makes the field meaningful may be lost in the process (not to mention the responsibility aspect of the role). I am not saying that you need to suffer doing a lot of tedious tasks (particularly in the data engineering part of the pipeline), but to merely be wary of people who misguidedly promise to automate everything, likely without having thought it through. Certain things will no doubt become automated, but the principles of data science and the core ideas of the craft will not. If automation was as easy as some people make it out to be, then no one would bother to learn calculus, for example, since there are programs out there that can undertake any calculus-related task, be it through processes of abstract mathematics or via a simulation.

Data science technologies will change in the next few years, and they will continue to change just like in any technology-related field. New theories will come out and make some of the existing methods obsolete. Yet, just like a robust generalization, if your understanding of the field is solid, no amount of change can shake that from you. You may need to adapt your way of performing certain tasks by adopting new methods and techniques, but you will still be able to offer value to an organization. Perhaps your soft skills (the part of your skill-set that is not technical or scientific) will become your key selling point, or maybe your analytical thinking will be what makes your an asset as a data scientist. Whatever the case, the more detached you become to the technologies themselves through a mature assimilation of the know-how and a more creative approach to dealing with the problems at hand, the better off you will be.

In this book, I tried to get this message across, along with the idea that the value of data science lies in what you can do, regardless of the tools you use. Mastery of the tools may be useful career-wise, but not the most essential part of the craft. This is why I did not emphasize the specifics of the various tools. After all, if there is one thing that remains relevant while time gradually makes our tools feel rusty and eventually obsolete, it is the data science *mindset*. Hopefully, this book has helped you gain a better glimpse of it and maybe even some insight on how you can expand your mind to include it. If that's the case, then you will be able to see meaning and elegance in the data as it gradually morphs into information, releasing the signal from the noise that surrounds it. If not, then you can at least draw some inspiration from all this, to find your own meaning in this great line of work and generate elegant insights in the process. It really is up to you.

Glossary

Accuracy (Rate): A commonly used metric for evaluating a classification system across all of the classes it predicts. It denotes the proportion of data points predicted correctly. Good for balanced datasets, but inaccurate for many other cases.

Anomaly Detection: A data science methodology that focuses on identifying abnormal data points. These belong to a class of interest and are generally significantly fewer than the data points of any other class of the dataset. Anomaly detection is sometimes referred to as novelty detection.

Area Under Curve (AUC) metric: A metric for a binary classifier's performance based on the ROC curve. It takes into account the confidence of the classifier and is generally considered a robust performance index.

Artificial Creativity: An application of AI where the AI system emulates human creativity in a variety of domains, including painting, poetry, music composition, and even problem-solving.

Artificial Intelligence (AI): A field of computer science dealing with the emulation of human intelligence using computer systems and its applications in a variety of domains. AI application in data science is a noteworthy and important factor in the field, and has been since the 2000s.

Artificial Neural Network (ANN): A graph-based artificial intelligence system which implements the universal approximator idea. Although ANNs started as a machine learning system focusing on predictive analytics, it has expanded over the years to include a large variety of tasks. They are comprised of a series of nodes called neurons, which are organized in layers. The first layer corresponds to all the inputs, the final layer to all the outputs, and the intermediary layers to a series of meta-features the ANN creates, each having a corresponding weight. ANNs are stochastic in nature, so every time they are trained over a set of data, the weights are noticeably different.

Association Rules: Empirical rules derived from a set of data aimed at connecting different entities in that data. Usually the data is unlabeled, and this methodology is part of data exploration.

Autoencoder: An artificial neural network system designed to represent codings in a very efficient manner. Autoencoders are a popular artificial intelligence system used for dimensionality reduction.

Big Data: Datasets that are so large and/or complex that it is virtually impossible to process with traditional data processing systems. Challenges include querying, analysis, capture, search, sharing, storage, transfer, and visualization. Ability to process big data could lead to decisions that are more confident, cost-effective, less risky, and have greater operational efficiency and are generally better overall.

Binning: Also known as discretization, binning refers to the transformation of a continuous variable into a discrete one.

Bootstrapping: A resampling method for performing sensitivity analysis, using the same sample repeatedly in order to get a better generalization of the population it represents and provide an estimate of the stability of the metric we have based on this sample.

Bug (in programming): An issue with an algorithm or its implementation. The process of fixing them is called debugging.

Business Intelligence (BI): A sub-field of data analytics focusing on basic data analysis of business-produced data for the purpose of improving the function of a business. BI is not the same as data science, though it does rely mainly on statistics as a framework.

Butterfly Effect: A phenomenon studied in chaos theory where a minute change in the original inputs of a system yields a substantial change in its outputs. Originally the butterfly effect only applied to highly complex systems (e.g. weather forecasts), but it has been observed in other domains, including data science.

Chatbot: An artificial intelligence system that emulates a person on a chat application. A chatbot takes its inputs text, processes it in an efficient manner, and yields a reply in text format. A chatbot may also carry out simple tasks based on its inputs. It can reply with a question in order to clarify the objective involved.

Classification: A very popular data science methodology under the predictive analytics umbrella. Classification aims to solve the problem of assigning a label (class) to a data point based on pre-existing knowledge of categorized data available in the training set.

Cloud (computing): A model that enables easy, on-demand access to a network of shareable computing resources that can be configured and customized to the application at hand. The cloud is a very popular resource in large-scale data analytics and a common resource for data science applications.

Clustering: A data exploration methodology that aims to find groupings in the data, yielding labels based on these groupings. Clustering is very popular when processing unlabeled data, and in some cases the labels it provides are used for classification afterwards.

Computer Vision: An application of artificial intelligence where a computer is able to discern a variety of visual inputs and effectively "see" many different real-world objects in real-time. Computer vision is an essential component of all modern robotics systems.

Confidence: A metric that aims to reflect the probability of another metric being correct. Usually it takes values between 0 and 1 (inclusive). Confidence is linked to statistics but it lends itself to heuristics and machine learning systems as well.

Confidentiality: The aspect of information security that has to do with keeping privileged information accessible to only those who should have access to it. Confidentiality is linked to privacy, though it encompasses other things, such as data anonymization and data security.

Confusion Matrix: A k-by-k matrix depicting the hits and misses of a classifier for a problem involving k classes. For a binary problem (involving two classes only), the matrix is comprised of various combinations of hits (trues) and misses (falses) referred to as true positives (cases of value 1 predicted as 1), true negatives (cases of value 0 predicted as 0), false positives (cases of value 0 predicted as 1), and false negatives (cases of value 1 predicted as 0). The confusion matrix is the basis for many evaluation metrics.

Correlation (coefficient): A metric of how closely related two continuous variables are in a linear manner.

Cost Function: A function for evaluating the amount of damage the total of all misclassifications amount to, based on individual costs pre-assigned to different kinds of errors. A cost function is a popular performance metric for complex classification problems.

Cross-entropy: A metric of how the addition of a variable affects the entropy of another variable.

Dark Data: Unstructured data, or any form of data where information is unusable. Dark data constitutes the majority of available data today.

Data Anonymization: The process of changing the data so that it cannot be used to identify any particular individual via the data that corresponds to him or her.

Data Analytics: A general term to describe the field involving data analysis as its main component. Data analytics is more general than data science, although the two terms are often used interchangeably.

Data Analyst: Anyone performing basic data analysis, usually using statistical approaches only, without any applicability on larger and/or more complex datasets. Data analysts usually rely on a spreadsheet application and/or basic statistics software for their work.

Data Anonymization: The process of removing or hiding personal identified information (PII) from the data analyzed.

Data Cleansing: An important part of data preparation, it involves removing corrupt or otherwise problematic data (e.g. unnecessary outliers) to ensure a stronger signal. After data cleansing, data starts to take the form of a dataset.

Data Discovery: The part of the data modeling stage in the data science pipeline that has to do with pinpointing patterns in the data that may lead to building a more relevant and more accurate model in the stages that follow.

Data Engineering: The first stage of the data science pipeline, responsible for cleaning, exploring, and processing the data so that it can become structured and useful in a model developed in the following stage of the pipeline.

Data Exploration: The part of the data engineering stage in the data science pipeline that has to do with getting a better understanding of the data through plots and descriptive statistics, as well as other methods, such as clustering. The visuals produced here are for the benefit of the data scientists involved, and may not be used in the later parts of the pipeline.

Data Frame: A data structure similar to a database table that is capable of containing different types of variables and performing advanced operations on its elements.

Data Governance: Managing data (particularly big data) in an efficient manner so that it is stored, transferred, and processed effectively. This is done with frameworks like Hadoop and Spark.

Data Learning: A crucial step in the data science pipeline, focusing on training and testing a model for providing insights and/or being part of a data product. Data learning is in the data modeling stage of the pipeline.

Data Mining: The process of finding patterns in data, usually in an automated way. Data mining is a data exploration methodology.

Data Modeling: A crucial stage in the data science pipeline, involving the creation of a model through data discovery and data learning.

Data Point: A single row in a dataset, corresponding to a single record of a database.

Data Preparation: A part of the data engineering stage in the data science pipeline focusing on setting up the data for the stages that follow. Data preparation involves data cleansing and normalization, among other things.

Data Representation: A part of the data engineering stage in the data science pipeline, focusing on using the most appropriate data types for the variables involved, as well as the coding of the relevant information in a set of features.

Data Science: The interdisciplinary field undertaking data analytics work on all kinds of data, with a focus on big data, for the purpose of mining insights and/or building data products.

Data Security: An aspect of confidentiality that involves keeping data secure from dangers and external threats (e.g. malware).

Data Structure: A collection of data points in a structured form used in programming as well as various parts of the data science pipeline.

Data Visualization: A part of the data science pipeline focusing on generating visuals (plots) of the data, the model's performance, and the insights found. The visuals produced here are mainly for the stakeholders of the project.

Database: An organized system for storing and retrieving data using a specialized language. The data can be structured or unstructured, corresponding to SQL and NoSQL databases. Accessing databases is a key process for acquiring data for a data science project.

Dataset: A structured data collection, usually directly usable in a data science model. Datasets may still have a lot to benefit from data engineering.

Deep Learning (DL): An artificial intelligence methodology employing large artificial neural networks to tackle highly complex problems. DL systems require a lot of data in order to yield a real advantage in terms of performance.

Dimensionality Reduction: A fairly common method in data analytics aiming to reduce the number of variables in a dataset. This can be accomplished either with meta-features, each one condensing the information of a number of features, or with the elimination of several features of low quality.

Discretization: See binning.

Encryption: The process of turning comprehensive and/or useful data into gibberish using a reversible process (encryption system) and a key. The latter is usually a password, a pass phrase, or a whole file. Encryption is a key aspect of data security.

Ensemble: A set of predictive analytics models bundled together in order to improve performance. An ensemble can be comprised of a set of models of the same category, but it can also consist of different model types.

Entropy: A metric of how much disorder exists in a given variable. This is defined for all kinds of variables.

Error Rate: Denotes the proportion of data points predicted incorrectly. Good for balanced datasets.

Ethics: A code of conduct for a professional. In data science, ethics revolves around things like data security, privacy, and proper handling of the insights derived from the data analyzed.

Experiment (data science related): A process involving the application of the scientific method on a data science question or problem.

F1 Metric: A popular performance metric for classification systems defined as the harmonic mean of precision and recall, and just like them, corresponds to a particular class. In cases of unbalanced datasets, it is more meaningful than accuracy rate. F1 belongs to a family of similar metrics, each one being a function of precision (P) and recall (R) in the form $F_\beta = (1 + \beta^2) (P * R) / (\beta^2 P + R)$, where β is a coefficient related to importance of precision in the particular aggregation metric F_β.

False Negative: In a binary classification problem, it is a data point of class 1, predicted as class 0. See confusion matrix for more context.

False Positive: In a binary classification problem, it is a data point of class 0, predicted as class 1. See confusion matrix for more context.

Feature: A processed variable capable of being used in a data science model. Features are generally the columns of a dataset.

Fitness Function: An essential part of most artificial intelligence systems, particularly those related to optimization. It depicts how close the system is getting to the desired outcome and helps it adjust its course accordingly.

Functional Programming: A programming paradigm where the programming language is focused on functions rather than objects or processes, thereby eliminating the need of a global variable space. Scripts of functional languages are modular and easy to debug.

Fusion: Usually used in conjunction with feature (e.g. feature fusion), this relates to the merging of a set of features into a single meta-feature that encapsulates all, or at least most, of the information in those features.

Fuzzy Logic: An artificial intelligence methodology that involves a flexible approach to the states a variable takes. For example, instead of having the states "hot" and "cold" in the variable "temperature," Fuzzy Logic allows for different levels of "hotness" making for a more human kind of reasoning. For more information about Fuzzy Logic check out MathWorks' webpage on the topic: http://bit.ly/2sBVQ3M.

Generalization: A key characteristic of a data science model where the system is able to handle data beyond its training set in a reliable way.

Git: A version control system that is popular among developers and data scientists alike. Unlike some other systems, Git is decentralized, making it more robust.

Github: A cloud-based repository for Git, accessible through a web browser.

Graph Analytics: A data science methodology making use of Graph Theory to tackle problems through the analysis of the relationships among the entities involved.

Hadoop: An established data governance framework for both managing and storing big data on a local computer cluster or a cloud setting.

HDFS: Short for Hadoop Distributed File System, HDFS enables the storage and access of data across several computers for easier processing through a data governance system (not just Hadoop).

Hypothesis: An educated guess related to the data at hand about a number of scenarios, such as the relationship between two variables or the difference between two samples. Hypotheses are tested via experiments to determine their validity.

Heuristic: An empirical metric or function that aims to provide some useful tool or insight, to facilitate a data science method or project.

IDE: Short for Integrated Development Environment, an IDE greatly facilitates the creation and running of scripts as well as their debugging.

Index of Discernibility: A family of heuristics created by the author that aim to evaluate features (and in some cases individual data points) for classification problems.

Information Distillation: A stage of the data science pipeline which involves the creation of data products and/or the deliverance of insights and visuals based on the analysis conducted in the project.

Insight: A non-obvious and useful piece of information derived from the use of a data science model on some data.

Internet of Things (IoT): A new technological framework that enables all kinds of devices (even common appliances) to have Internet connectivity. This greatly enhances the amount of data collected and usable in various aspects of everyday life.

Julia: A modern programming language of the functional programming paradigm comprised of characteristics for both high-level and low-level languages. Its ease of use, high speed, scalability, and sufficient amount of packages make it a robust language well-suited for data science.

Jupyter: A popular browser-based IDE for various data science languages, such as Python and Julia.

Kaggle: A data science competition site focusing on the data modeling part of the pipeline. It also has a community and a job board.

K-fold Cross Validation: A fundamental data science experiment technique for building a model and ensuring that it has a reliable generalization potential.

Labels: A set of values corresponding to the points of a dataset, providing information about the dataset's structure. The latter takes the form of classes, often linked to classification applications. The variable containing the labels is typically used as the target variable of the dataset.

Layer: A set of neurons in an artificial neural network. Inner layers are usually referred to as hidden layers and consist mainly of meta-features created by the system.

Library: See package.

Machine Learning (ML): A set of algorithms and programs that aim to process data without relying on statistical methods. ML is fast, and some methods of it are significantly more accurate than the corresponding statistical ones, while the assumptions they make about the data are fewer. There is a noticeable overlap between ML and artificial intelligence systems designed for data science.

Minimum Squared Error (MSE): A popular metric for evaluating the performance of regression systems by taking the difference of each prediction with the target variable (error) and squaring it. The model having the smallest such squared error is usually considered the optimal one.

Mentoring: The process of someone knowledgeable and adept in a field sharing his experience and advice with others newer to the field. Mentoring can be a formal endeavor or something circumstantial, depending on the commitment of the people involved.

Metadata: Data about a piece of data. Examples of metadata are: timestamps, geolocation data, data about the data's creator, and notes.

Meta-features (super features or synthetic features): High quality features that encapsulate large amounts of information, usually represented in a series of conventional features. Meta-features are either synthesized in an artificial intelligence system or created through dimensionality reduction.

Monte Carlo Simulation: A simulation technique for estimating probabilities around a phenomenon, without making assumptions about the phenomenon itself. Monte Carlo simulations have a variety of applications, from estimating functions to sensitivity analysis.

Natural Language Processing (NLP): A text analytics methodology focusing on categorizing the various parts of speech for a more in-depth analysis of the text involved.

Neuron: A fundamental component of an artificial neural network, usually representing an input (feature), a meta-feature, or an output. Neurons are organized in layers.

Non-negative Matrix Factorization (NMF or NNMF): An algebraic technique for splitting a matrix containing only positive values and zeros into a couple of matrices that correspond to meaningful data, useful for recommender systems.

Normalization: The process of transforming a variable so that it is of the same range as the other variables in a dataset. This is done through statistical methods primarily and is part of the data engineering stage in the data science pipeline.

NoSQL Database: A database designed for unstructured data. Such a database is also able to handle structured data too, as NoSQL stands for Not Only SQL.

Novelty Detection: See anomaly detection.

Object-Oriented Programming (OOP): A programming paradigm where all structures, be it data or code, are handled as objects. In the case of data, objects can have various fields (referred to as attributes), while when referring to code, objects can have various procedures (referred to as methods).

Optimization: An artificial intelligence process aimed at finding the best value of a function (usually referred to as the fitness function), given a set of restrictions. Optimization is key in all modern data science systems.

Outlier: An abnormal data point, often holding particular significance. Outliers are not always extreme values, as they can exist near the center of the dataset as well.

Over-fitting: Making the model too specialized to a particular dataset. Its main characteristic is great performance for the training set and poor performance for any other dataset.

Package: A set of programs designed for a specific set of related tasks, sharing the same data structures and freely available to the users of a given programming language. Packages may require other packages in order to function, which are called dependencies. Once installed, the package can be imported in the programming language and used in scripts.

Paradigm: An established way of doing things, as well as the set of similar methodologies in a particular field. Paradigms change very slowly, but when they do, they are accompanied by a change of mindset and often new scientific theory.

Pipeline: Also known as workflow, it is a conceptual process involving a variety of steps, each one of which can be comprised of several other processes. A pipeline is essential for organizing the tasks needed to perform any complex procedure (often non-linear) and is very applicable in data science (this application is known as the data science pipeline).

Population: The theoretical total of all the data points for a given dataset. As this is not accessible, an approximate representation of the population is used through sampling.

Precision: A performance metric for classification systems focusing on a particular class. It is defined as the ratio of the true positives of that class over the total number of predictions related to that class.

Predictive Analytics: A set of methodologies of data science related to the prediction of certain variables. It includes a variety of techniques, such as classification, regression, time-series analysis, and more. Predictive analytics are a key data science methodology.

Privacy: An aspect of confidentiality that involves keeping certain pieces of information private.

Recall: A performance metric for classification systems focusing on a particular class. It is defined as the ratio of the true positives of that class over the total number of data points related to that class.

Recommender System (RS): Also known as a recommendation engine, a RS is a data science system designed to provide a set of similar entities to the ones described in a given dataset based on the known values of the features of these entities. Each entity is represented as a data point in the RS dataset.

Regression: A very popular data science methodology under the predictive analytics umbrella. Regression aims to solve the problem of predicting the values of a continuous variable corresponding to a set of inputs based on pre-existing knowledge of similar data, available in the training set.

Resampling: The process of sampling repeatedly in order to ensure more stable results in a question or a model. Resampling is a popular methodology for sensitivity analysis.

ROC Curve: A curve representing the trade-off between true positives and false positives for a binary classification problem, useful for evaluating the classifier used. The ROC curve is usually a zig-zag line depicting the true positive rate for each false positive rate value.

Sample: A limited portion of the data available, useful for building a model and (ideally) representative of the population it belongs to.

Sampling: The process of acquiring a sample of a population using a specialized technique. Sampling must be done properly to ensure that the resulting sample is representative of the population studied. Sampling needs to be random and unbiased.

Scala: A functional programming language, very similar to Java, that is used in data science. The big data framework Spark is based on Scala.

Scientific Process: The process of forming a hypothesis, processing the available data, and reaching a conclusion in a rigorous and reproducible manner. Conclusions are not 100% valid. Every scientific field, including data science, applies the scientific process.

Sensitivity Analysis: The process of establishing the stability of a result or how prone a model's performance is to change, if the initial data is different. It involves several methods, such as resampling and "what if" questions.

Sentiment Analysis: A text analytics method that involves inferring the sentiment polarity of a piece of text using its words and some metadata that may be attached to it.

Signal: A piece of valuable information within a collection of data. Insights derived from the analysis of the data tend to reflect the various signals identified in the data.

Spark: A big data framework focusing on managing and processing data through a series of specialized modules. Spark does not handle storing data, just handling it.

SQL: Short for Structured Query Language, SQL is a basic programming language used in databases containing structured data. Although it does not apply to big data, many modern databases are using query languages based on SQL.

Statistical Test: A test for establishing relationships between two samples based on statistics concepts. Each statistical test has a few underlying assumptions behind it.

Statistics: A sub-field of mathematics that focuses on data analysis using probability theory, a variety of distributions, and tests. Statistics involves a series of assumptions about the data involved. There are two main types of statistics: descriptive and inferential. The former deals with describing the data at hand, while the latter with making predictions using statistical models.

Steganography: The process of hiding a file in another much larger file (usually a photo, an audio clip, or a video) using specialized software. The process does not change how the file seems or sounds. Steganography is a data security methodology.

Stochastic: Something that is probabilistic in nature (i.e. not deterministic). Stochastic processes are common in most artificial intelligence systems and other advanced machine learning systems.

Structured Data: Data that has a form that enables it to be used in all kinds of data analytics models. Structured data usually takes the form of a dataset.

Target Variable: The variable of a dataset that is the target of a predictive analytics system, such as a classifier or a regressor.

Text Analytics: The sub-field of data science that focuses on all text-related problems. It includes natural language processing (NLP), among other things.

Testing Set: The part of the dataset that is used for testing a predictive analytics model after it has been trained and before it is deployed. The testing set usually corresponds to a small portion of the original dataset.

Training Set: The part of the dataset that is used for training a predictive analytics model before it is tested and deployed. The training set usually corresponds to the largest portion of the original dataset.

Transfer Function: The function applied on the output of a neuron in an artificial neural network.

Time-series Analysis: A data science methodology aiming to tackle dynamic data problems, where the values of a target variable change over time. In time-series analysis, the target variable is also used as an input in the model.

True Negative: In a binary classification problem, it is a data point of class 0, predicted as such. See confusion matrix for more context.

True Positive: In a binary classification problem, it is a data point of class 1, predicted as such. See confusion matrix for more context.

Unstructured Data: Data that lacks any structural frame (e.g. free-form text) or data from various sources. The majority of big data is unstructured data and requires significant processing before it is usable in a model.

Versatilist: A professional who is an expert in one skill, but has a variety of related skills, usually in a tech-related field, allowing him to perform several roles in an organization. Data scientists tend to have a versatilist mentality.

Version Control System (VCS): A programming tool aiming to keep various versions of your documents (usually programming scripts and data files) accessible and easy to maintain, allowing for variants of them to co-exist with the original ones. VCS are great for collaboration of various people on the same files.

Index

AI systems
   and heuristics, 148
   types of, 157–61
AI-based methods, 56–58
Algorithms
   graph, 48–50
Amazon Echo, 55
Amazon's MXnet, 179
Analytica, 71
Anomaly detection, 40–41
Artificial creativity, 56, 60, 163
Artificial Intelligence (AI), 18, 24
   importance of, 156–57
   in data science, 155
   trends in, 176
Artificial Neural Networks (ANN), 54,
   157, 166
Association rules, 46
Autoencoders, 159, 166
Automated data exploration, 59
Automated data exploration methods,
   45
Automatic translation systems, 164
Big data, 13, 15–17, 24, 176
   4 V's of, 16–17
Bootstrap method, 109
Bootstrapping, 109–10
Business intelligence, 14
Butterfly effect, 40, 108–9, 114
Chatbots, 55, 60, 162–63
Classification, 38, 40
Classification methodology
   model for, 138–39

Classifier, 38
Clustering methods, 44, 46–47
Collaborative filtering method, 42, 43,
   44
Collaborative projects, 181–82
Computer vision, 161, 166
Conditional Random Field, 53
Confidence, 101–3, 105
Confidentiality, 168, 170, 171, 174
Content-based systems, 42, 43
Convolution layers, 159
Convolutional Neural Networks
   (CNNs), 166
Cosine distance, 43
CVS, 78
D3.js, 73–74
Data
   pairing with model, 137–38
Data analytics software, 70–72
Data anonymization, 170, 174
Data discovery, 30, 35
Data engineering, 20, 24, 26, 35
Data exploration method, 28, 35, 45, 46,
   49
Data frame, 27
Data governance, 75, 80
Data governance software, 74–75
Data learning, 31, 35
Data mining method, 45–46
Data modeling, 21, 24, 29–30, 35
Data preparation, 27, 35
Data product creation, 32–33, 35
Data representation, 28–29, 35

Data science, 13, 24
  and AI, 155, 161
  and AI consideration, 165
  future trends and, 175–83
  heuristics in, 145, 149
  methodologies in, 37–58
  programming languages for, 64–67
Data science ethics, 167
  importance of, 167–68
Data science pipeline, 34
Data science process, 24
  mistakes in, 125, 131
Data science professionals
  need for, 22–23
Data science research, 180
Data science technologies, 185
Data science vs. business intelligence
  vs. statistics, 13
Data scientists
  continuous education and, 181
  functions of, 20–21
  inability of, 21–22
  need for, 20, 22–23
  tools and software of, 61
  versatility of, 179–80
Data security, 171–72, 174
Database platforms, 61
Databases, 62
  and data science, 79
Deep learning networks, 158–59, 166
Dimensionless space, 48
Discrete target variable
  and classification, 38
Distance functions, 47
DL networks, 178
Ensemble, 151
Ensemble setting, 139
Entity recognition, 53
Ethics, 173–74
  data science, 167

  importance of, 167–68
Experiment conclusions
  sensitivity analysis and, 107
Experiments, 97
  and predictive analytics system, 100–101
  constructing, 98–99
  evaluating the results, 103–4
Extreme learning machines (ELMs), 160
Feature creation, 127
Feature evaluation
  and heuristics, 150
Feature set, 90–91
Fuzzy logic systems, 160
GenEx, 54
Git, 77
Github, 78, 182
Global sensitivity analysis, 109
GPUs, 178
Graph
  composition of, 47
Graph algorithms, 48–50
Graph analysis, 54, 59
Graph analytics, 47
Graph modeling, 50
Graph processing, 50
Graph-based databases, 63
Graphs, 59
  uses of, 50
Hadoop, 75–76, 178
Heuristic
  anatomy of, 151–53
Heuristics, 145–46, 153–54
  and AI systems, 148
  and feature evaluation, 150
  applications and, 151
  in data science, 145, 149
  solving problems with, 146–48
High-level mistakes
  coping with, 135–36

Hypothesis, 85–86, 95

Inductive/deductive classifiers, 38

Infographic
  on big data, 17

Information distillation, 21, 24, 32, 35

Insight, deliverance, and visualization
  of findings, 33, 35

Internet Movie Database (IMDb), 42

Internet of Things (IoT), 176

Jaccard distance, 43

Jackknife, 110–11

JavaScript library, 73

Julia, 65, 67
  libraries for, 69–70

KPSpotter, 54

Latent Dirichlet Allocation (LDA), 52

Libraries, 68–70

Licensing matters, 172–73, 174

Local sensitivity analysis, 112

Machine Learning (ML), 18, 24

Machine learning processes
  heuristics and, 149

Massive Open Online Courses
  (MOOC's), 23

Mathematica, 72, 74

MATLAB, 71

Mentor, 132
  value of, 131

Mentoring, 182

Minimum Spanning Tree, 49

Mistakes, 132
  common types, 126–29
  high-level, 135–36

Mistakes vs. bugs, 125–26

Model
  and data pairing, 137–38
  choosing, 129–30, 136, 140–41

Monte Carlo, 111

Natural Language Processing (NLP), 51,
  59, Error! Not a valid bookmark in
  entry on page 59

Navigation systems, 164

Neo4j, 50

NLP methods, 54

NMF algorithm, 44

Non-negative matrix factorization
  (NMF or NNMF), 43, 44

NoSQL databases, 62–63

Novelty detection, 40–41

Null Hypothesis, 86

Object-Oriented Programming (OOP),
  177

Octave, 71

Open-source programming platforms,
  79

Outlier prediction, 41

Packages, 68–70

Parallelization, 178

Permutation methods, 110

Pipeline, 197

Plot.ly, 73

Pooling layers, 159

Predictive analytics, 37, 58

Predictive analytics method, 43

Predictive analytics methodology, 41

Privacy, 168–69, 174

Programming bugs, 117–22, 122
  common types, 119–22
  considerations on, 122
  coping with, 133–35
  understanding, 117–18
  where they are, 117–18

Programming languages, 79
  choosing, 67
  for Data Science, 64–67
  Julia, 65
  Python, 65–66

Programming paradigms, 177

Python, 65–66
  libraries for, 68
Query Language (SQL), 62
Questions, 95
  and common cases, 86
  and data science, 83
  and for predicting variable, 89–90
  not to ask, 94
  relationships and, 87–88
  what to ask, 84–85
R, 66
Randomization technique, 110
Recommendation systems, 42
Recommender systems, 42, 43, 58, 137
Recurrent Neural Networks (RNNs),
  166
Regression, 39
Regularization, 44
Resampling methods, 109, 114
Rules
  application of, 38
Scala, 67
Scalability, 152
Scilab, 71
Sensitivity analysis, 107, 112–13, 113
  importance of, 107
Sentiment analysis, 51, 53, 60
Slack, 182
Spark, 75, 76
SQL-based databases, 62

Statistics, 14
Stopwords, 53
Storm, 76
Tableau, 74
TCP tunneling technique, 169
Tensor Processing Units, 178
Text prediction, 41–42
Text summarization, 53–54, 60
Time-series analysis, 40
Topic extraction, 60
Topic Extraction/Modeling, 52
Transductive classifiers, 38
Turney, 54
Utility matrix, 42, 44
Value
  of big data, 17
Variety, 17, 24
Velocity, 16, 24
Veracity, 17, 24
Versatilist data scientist, 179–80
Version control systems (VCS) software,
  77–79, 80
Virtual private network (VPN), 169
Visualization options, 79
Visualization software, 73
Volume, 16, 24
WolframAlpha, 74
Workflow. See Pipeline
Yahoo, 169